"A beautifully constructed SENCO guide sharing the honest reality of the role with the heart, diligence and passion of those who've lived it woven throughout. Highly insightful with practical approaches and ideas. An absolute must for *all* SENCOs, both new and experienced."
— **Kate Williams**, *SEND Consultant and Qualified SENCO*

"Being a SENCO is one of the most fulfilling, but challenging roles in education. The approach Adam and Maxine take in their book is to make you consider the factors that put children and young people at the forefront of our practice. This book is essential reading for any prospective or practicing SENCOs, making the role accessible and chunking everything you need to consider. It gives practical advice based on theory and is a thoroughly enjoyable read."
— **John Holt**, *Local Authority SEND Lead*

"An accessible, eye-opening read about the extensive, often invisible, work of SENCOs. A stark reminder that meeting the needs of young people with SEND cannot solely be the role of the SENCO, it is paramount that there is a shared sense of responsibility between all who come into contact with students with barriers to learning in educational settings. Written by experts in the field, the authors use their extensive knowledge and experience to offer thoughtful insights and creative ideas around inclusive and adaptive teaching practices, such as 'dynamic risk-assessments' and 'pre-mortem' thinking. As highlighted in the book, adapting to ever changing cohorts, and the ever-increasing need for inclusivity in the classroom, is a challenge for all educational providers, regardless of the setting."
— **Jeanette Davies**, *Director of Music and Head of the Creative Arts Faculty, Birkenhead High School Academy (GDST – Girls Day School Trust)*

# The Secret Life of SENCOs

Practical Insights on Inclusion
and Specialist Provision

**Adam Boddison and Maxine O'Neill**

Routledge
Taylor & Francis Group

LONDON AND NEW YORK

Designed cover image: © Getty Images

First published 2025
by Routledge
4 Park Square, Milton Park, Abingdon, Oxon OX14 4RN

and by Routledge
605 Third Avenue, New York, NY 10158

*Routledge is an imprint of the Taylor & Francis Group, an informa business*

*British Library Cataloguing-in-Publication Data*
A catalogue record for this book is available from the British Library

ISBN: 978-1-032-63479-1 (hbk)
ISBN: 978-1-032-63478-4 (pbk)
ISBN: 978-1-032-63480-7 (ebk)

DOI: 10.4324/9781032634807

Typeset in Helvetica
by Apex CoVantage, LLC

This book is dedicated to Mum.
A force for good in making the world a better place for so many children.
Probably the reason why we both ended up working with children ourselves.
A beacon of hope whose light faded far too soon.
Long may her inspiration and vision live on through us.

# Contents

*List of Figures, Tables and Boxes*                                              xii
*Have a HEART!*                                                                   xiv
*Foreword by Tina Emery OBE*                                                      xvi
*Introduction*                                                                   xviii

**1    Evolution of the SENCO Role**                                              **1**

What Do We Mean by 'the SENCO'?                                                   1
The Evolution of the SENCO Role                                                   2
The Current Iteration of the SENCO Role                                           3
    SENCO Responsibilities                                    4
    SENCO Workload and Administration                         4
    SENCOs as Strategic Leaders                               6
    Phase-Specific SENCO Variations                           7
    SENCOs as Pastoral Leaders or Drivers of Quality-First Teaching    8
    SENCO Ethics                                              8
    The Depth, Breadth and Reach of the SENCO Role           12
    Going Beyond the Statutory Requirements                   14
    The SEND Governor                                         14
Other Developments Related to the SENCO Role                                     17
Conclusion                                                                       18

**2    The Alternatives to School Exclusions**                                    **19**

Exclusions: The National Picture                                                  19
No Option but to Exclude?                                                         21
    Responding to the Immediate Situation                     22
    Headteacher Red Lines                                     26
    Developing the School's Approach Over Time                28
The Duality of Behaviour Management and Parenting                                 33
The 'Hope School' Approach                                                        34
    HEARTS                                                    37
    Zero Exclusions                                           37
    Example of the Four Rs in Practice                        38
    Zero Exclusion Strategies                                 39
Red Lines – Stakeholder Perspectives                                             40
    The Child                                                 40
    The School Community                                      41
    Parents and Carers                                        41
    Staff                                                     41
The 'Nisai Approach' to Respond to School Exclusion (by Laura Brown, Nisai Group)    43
    Academic Exclusion                                        43
    Social Exclusion                                          44
    Equality and Equity                                       45
Conclusion                                                                       47

**3  Data for Delivery**                                              **49**

Typical Data Usage by SENCOs                                           50
    Conspicuous Omissions                          51
Further Ideas for Data Usage by SENCOs                                 52
    SEND Identification Data                       52
    Summary of Other Data Sources for SEND         55
    Gov.UK Open Data Hub                           56
    Provision Maps                                 56
    Apples and Pears                               56
Data Literacy for SENCOs                                               56
    Data Familiarisation                           57
    Visuals for Communication                      57
    Discuss the Data                               60
    Learn, Unlearn and Relearn                     62
    Basics of Excel                                62
Other Data Concepts                                                    68
Artificial Intelligence in Schools                                     69
    ChatGPT's Top Ten for Inclusive Schools        72
Conclusion                                                             73

**4  Lessons Learned, Lessons Applied**                                **75**

The Benefit of Hindsight                                               75
    Getting Stuck and Trying Things                75
    Career Development                             76
    Getting Practical and Tactical                 76
    Going the Extra Mile                           79
The Toll of the SENCO Role                                             80
    Leaning on Family and Colleagues               80
    Professional Support and Clinical Supervision  80
    Mindset                                        81
    The SENCO Work-Life Balance                    82
Relationships                                                          84
    Relationships in General                       84
    Relationships with Parents and Carers          84
    Relationships with Colleagues                  85
SENCOs and Ofsted Inspections                                          86
    Data and the Big Picture                       86
    Case Studies                                   87
    Practical Advice                               87
Good Intentions                                                        88
Conclusion                                                             89

**5  Individual Stories**                                              **91**

Bobby                                                                  91
    Background and Context                         91
    Responses Over Time                            91
    Bobby's New School                             91
    Reflections                                    92
Harry                                                                  92
    Background and Context                         92
    Lockdown                                       93
    The Developing Relationship Between School and Home  93

Escalation of Behaviours and Consequences 93
A Different Approach 94
Reflections 94
Mary, Zora, Clare, Savita, Zoey, Grey and Gracey 94
Background and Context 94
Mary 95
Zora 95
The Other Children in the Group 95
Reflections 96
Conclusion 96

*Glossary of Acronyms* 97
*References* 99
*Index* 105

# Figures, Tables and Boxes

## Figures

2.1 The number of schools in England with zero permanent exclusions and zero suspensions (per term)  20
2.2 The proportion of permanent exclusions over time who are pupils with SEND  20
2.3 Suspensions of young children over time  21
2.4 Five important steps to be included as part of the immediate response to a dysregulated pupil displaying behaviours that may lead to an exclusion  22
2.5 Power and interest matrix  24
2.6 The four parenting styles  33
2.7 Equality, equity and liberation  36
2.8 Rising tides concept of ordinarily available provision  37
2.9 The four Rs  38
2.10 Nisai breakdown of needs (2022/2023)  46
3.1 Analysis by primary areas of need – Lady Videtta High School  54
3.2 Five steps towards data literacy  57
3.3 Termly increase in average reading age for different pupil groups  59
3.4 Termly increase in average reading age and impact of intervention on average reading age for different pupil groups  60
3.5 Impact of literacy intervention on target group  61
3.6 Example of a 'SEND chart of the month'  61
3.7 Raw marks from pupils' numeracy assessments  63
3.8 Basic addition formula on Excel  63
3.9 Creating a bar chart on Excel  64
3.10 The chart design tab in Excel  64
3.11 Creating a stacked bar chart in Excel  65
3.12 Example of a stacked bar chart  65
3.13 Turning on filtering in Excel  65
3.14 Highlighting cells in Excel ready for sorting  66
3.15 Example of a sorted list in Excel  66
3.16 Getting started with conditional formatting in Excel  67
3.17 Conditional formatting boxes in Excel  67

## Tables

2.1 Example of a RACI matrix  33
3.1 Reflection questions about the proportion of learners with SEND  53
3.2 Analysis by primary areas of need – Lady Videtta High School  54
3.3 Class reading ages pre- and post-literacy intervention  58
3.4 Average increase in reading age for different pupil groups  59

## Boxes

1.1 Why do teachers choose to become a SENCO?  5
1.2 The challenge of squeezed school budgets  7

| | | |
|---|---|---:|
| 1.3 | To label or not to label? | 9 |
| 1.4 | Should the SENCO be a SEND expert? | 10 |
| 1.5 | SEND magnets | 13 |
| 1.6 | The SEND Governor role description | 15 |
| 2.1 | Charlie's situation | 21 |
| 2.2 | At what point might a victim become a perpetrator? | 28 |
| 2.3 | An example of recognising antecedents to inform inclusion tactics | 29 |
| 2.4 | Building a movement break into the lesson | 30 |
| 2.5 | Pre-mortems for identifying and mitigating risks | 31 |
| 2.6 | Perceptions of SEND: superpower analogy | 35 |
| 2.7 | Primary school case studies | 42 |
| 3.1 | Using ChatGPT to write a SEND strategy | 70 |
| 4.1 | Sharing the administrative burden – getting others involved in SEND processes | 77 |
| 4.2 | Taking a pupil off the SEND register | 78 |
| 4.3 | Passion and politeness are not mutually exclusive | 79 |
| 4.4 | Trauma-informed approaches to SEND provision | 81 |
| 4.5 | Intervening to prevent the self-fulfilling prophecy | 81 |
| 4.6 | Appointing a Deputy SENCO | 83 |
| 4.7 | Is the EHC plan a 'golden ticket'? | 86 |
| 4.8 | Celebrating the small things (which are also the big things!) | 87 |
| 4.9 | Behaviour as a communication of need | 88 |

# Have a HEART!

*"In my day the kids had respect*
*The teachers were people to fear.*
*You did as they asked in the classroom*
*Or they'd haul you out by the ear!"*

This is the belief of so many,
Fight fire with fire in school.
But does it really help the child
to berate them for breaking a rule?

Because life in school is much more.
We offer above what you think.
We know more and more about damage,
Which has led us all to re-think.

We were open to finding out more,
How could we help these young things?
We looked at the background of their lives.
Realised what attachment and trauma brings.

But where to begin – what to do?
No-one really knew where to start.
Then a group of people who cared enough
Got together with the help of HEARTS.

To meet and learn new things.
To share what made us despair.
With serious reading to help us
we were optimistic we could repair.

Schools had to become safe places,
Where children could thrive, despite . . .
. . . the things they'd experienced in life . . .
a loss . . . a punch or a fight.

To begin, some people thought it soft,
The kids were ruling the roost!
They wanted them to pay for their errors,
The niceness must be reduced!

But we learnt and we shared what we knew.
Saw the reasons for the angry voice.
We talked about the harmful damage.
How the child had been given no choice.

So, when the chair flew across the room,
When he left a lesson in a rage.
We knew shouting was never the answer,
We'd talk and begin to engage.

What was the cause of the problem?
Where would we turn for advice?
HEARTS guided and helped us
Their assistance was clear and concise.

We began to see some change.
The staff, feeling more at ease,
understanding why an incident happened
not shouting, but using their expertise.

The boundaries remained in the schools,
natural consequences became the norm.
The children accepted the change, so well
They were happy to run with reform.

But the biggest change was in us,
Those who had turned to HEARTS.
Our understanding of these children
was immeasurable in considerable parts.

Their ACEs were damaging their chances,
In life, of that we were sure.
We needed to give them a future,
Ensure life chances were secure.

So hats off everyone with HEARTS.
For joining us on this tour.
For helping us understand . . .
. . . to help these children restore . . .

. . . their hearts and minds for the future
To return their chances in life.
So the path they walk will be gentle
Diverted from trouble and strife.

*Terry Cotton*
*October 2023*

# Foreword by Tina Emery OBE

I have been asked to write a foreword to this book around what makes a good SENCO. It can be hard to describe someone in a role that is something different to everyone.

I have worked alongside quite a few SENCOs in my time, and as a parent of two children with SEND, I have also been on what can be described as 'the receiving end'.

My experience of both is that often the SENCO is a person who genuinely wants to improve the school experience of a child and young person and their families. The role over the years has morphed into something a retired SENCO wouldn't necessarily recognise today, but if they were honest, they would probably say it isn't unexpected.

The SENCO role is an interesting one and varied. Often there are discussions of whether a SENCO should sit on their school's leadership team, and it is an individual choice, but I do think an understanding of the school's SEN budget is helpful, especially as your role to coordinate SEN provision will be driven by your school's SEN budget.

Of course, some SENCOs will be in several schools. School budgets and small schools are the catalysts for this drive to have a SENCO in school for just one day a week. This, I think, can be particularly hard to manage.

In a school I once saw a SENCO who was still a classroom teacher, with a small team of SEN support staff. The team delivered the interventions, worked one to one with families and prepared the paperwork for the educational psychologist or any other person coming in to school. And whilst it sounded luxurious, and it definitely does, it worked well, because the SENCO was doing what they should be doing – coordinating.

The SENCO should not be seen as the one person solely responsible for SEND. That builds the role into something that is unachievable and can lead to professional burnout.

Despite the varied makeup of what makes a good SENCO in a school and the variations of how many days they are in a role, how many days they teach, etc., there are some fundamental essentials to this role, which I think are key.

Communication is vital. A parent carer will only come to you when they want questions answered or when they are worried about something. Far too many conversations with parent carers occur when they come to you with their concerns and often view SENCOs as the only person that can fix it. This of course is not true. SENCOs are amazing people, but they do not have a magic wand to fix things, unfortunately.

Communication is not limited to just between the parent carers, you and the child, but actually it is a whole school approach, which for me is from the moment the child wakes up to the moment the child goes to bed. This is where your role as part of the senior leadership team comes in.

Situations arise and the families have to retell their story more than once, because conversations occur in silos. As soon as a parent carers retell their story for what seems like the tenth time to them, because the situation has escalated, trust erodes. This in turn makes your job difficult and the jobs of those who support you.

By ensuring that you and your role are supported well, you should make sure people in your school, no matter their role, understand all things SEND. Who should they signpost to, is there a graduated response or ordinarily available toolkits in your local area? If there are, signpost staff and parents to them. Do they know of the Local Offer? If not, why not? Two very simple avenues of support that can be used by parents, young people and practitioners and staff alike. And of course, your local parent carer forums. I wouldn't be here writing this if it weren't for them. Parent Carer Forums can signpost everyone to most things SEND in your local area.

I have, over the years, experienced decision-making panels within my local area. SENCOs were part of that process, and if your local area has the opportunity for you to join them for even one session, you should. It gives you an insight to what your local area is looking for, when applying for Education, Health and Care Needs Assessments.

And lastly, whilst I am conscious that I could have written way more than I have, I didn't want to overwhelm you. You are either thinking of exploring this role more, you have just taken up this role or you have been doing it for a while but wanted a refresh, I want to say this.

Thank you.

There will be days (as you know from teaching) where you will be frustrated. You may experience frustration given to you by people you are dealing with, by the systems in hand or by life in general. But you are part of a unique group of people that play such an important role within a school and to families. In case it's not been said today, we appreciate all you do.

Tina Emery OBE

# Introduction

## SENCOs Operating Under the Radar

This book is about the role of the SENCO (Special Educational Needs Coordinator). It is about the aspects of the role that are visible, but also the aspects that are 'invisible' because they are hidden in plain sight. The reality is that the vast majority of SENCOs routinely go above and beyond what is formally required of them. Many do this additional work under the radar and often in their own time as they know that going the extra mile can be transformational for the children and young people they are working with.

It is worth clarifying that the additional work being described here is not a 'nice to have', but an 'essential' for these children and young people to have their needs met. It is described as 'extra' because it is not definitively part of the SENCO role, but SENCOs do it because they know they are well placed (in some cases best placed) to provide what is needed. For children and young people accessing provision across health, education and social care, it can often be the SENCO who is uniquely placed to ensure that nothing falls through the cracks and that everything that is needed is put into place.

This characteristic of doing more than what is written in the job description is not unique to SENCOs. It is also true of lots of teachers and school leaders, and arguably many of the professionals working in the education sector. However, the additional invisible work being done by SENCOs is different to that being done by the wider education workforce for three distinct reasons.

Firstly, the additional invisible work being done by SENCOs is not well understood at a system level. The expectations that SENCOs put on themselves (or that are put on them by other stakeholders) can vary dramatically from school to school depending on the specific context and the experience of the individual SENCO. Whilst teaching roles and school leadership roles can differ between schools, there is arguably a greater level of consistency across these roles than across SENCO roles.

Secondly, SENCOs are typically responsible for coordinating provision for those children and young people with the most complex needs. This requires a depth of understanding at the individual pupil level that is distinct to the SENCO role compared to other school-based roles. Similarly, SENCOs have to engage regularly with a wide variety of external stakeholders, from parents and carers to social workers and health professionals.

Thirdly, it is the SENCO role that has been most acutely impacted by the tightening budgets and other resource limitations in the education system over recent years. For example, staffing is the most significant cost in most (likely all) schools. In small primary schools, there is limited scope for reducing staffing costs as each class needs a teacher, so reducing the time available for the SENCO role has too often been a go-to strategy. At the same time, the volume and complexity of needs in schools has been increasing. Higher-quality healthcare has resulted in children with complex needs having higher life expectancies than might have been the case historically and therefore accessing education for longer. This combination of factors means there is more for SENCOs to do, but with fewer resources.

Similarly, schools looking to reduce staffing costs may look to decrease the number of teaching assistants or learning support staff they employ. Once again, this has a disproportionate impact on the SENCO role, since it is these staff who typically deliver small group interventions and one-to-one provision for pupils with SEND (special educational needs and/or disabilities).

Reducing the allocated SENCO time or the number of teaching assistants in a school is folly as a strategic approach since, although it reduces costs in the short term, it is likely to increase costs over time. Failing to identify and meet needs early will create widening gaps between pupils with SEND and pupils without SEND, resulting in more specialist (and costly) provision being required at a later stage.

In summary, the SENCO role is different from other roles in schools. SENCOs are routinely doing more under the radar and in their own time to ensure that children's needs are met, but this is not well understood at a system level. The growing complexity of needs of children and young people in schools combined with unhelpful evolutions of education policy are disproportionately impacting the SENCO role. Being the SENCO can be a lonely role as there is typically only one per school. It is not always easy for SENCOs to know how other SENCOs in other schools are undertaking the role. More specifically, SENCOs may not be sure whether the additional unseen work they are doing in their school is typical of what SENCOs are doing in other schools.

This is where *The Secret Life of SENCOs* comes in. This book is written to share the wisdom and experience of individual SENCOs with the entire SENCO community. It provides practical insights on inclusion and specialist provision. From the things SENCOs wish they had known at the outset of their career to the best and worst decisions they have made, this book shines a light on the professional inner secrets of SENCOs. Very specifically, it explores alternatives to school exclusion, examines ways of using data to improve inclusion and shares the inspirational stories of individual learners with SEND. *The Secret Life of SENCOs* aims to transform how SENCOs execute their role by combining the benefit of hindsight with the luxury of insight to provide the privilege of foresight.

## Why This Book? Why Now?

Many excellent books have been written about the role of the SENCO in recent years, so it would be fair to ask what is different about this book. Whilst most of the books written for SENCOs have focused on how to undertake the statutory duties of the role, this book extends the remit further to explore aspects of the role that are too often unseen.

In addition to drawing on interviews and discussions with more than 100 SENCOs that have taken place over the past five years, this book also draws on insights from school leaders and those working in specialist provision, thereby providing a more holistic and rounded view of the role. Where necessary, the confidentiality of the identities of those who participated in the research for this book has been maintained through strategies such as

- adapting some contextual aspects,
- using pseudonyms, and
- deliberately conflating similar stories.

All participants provided consent for their contributions to be used in this way. Although the sample of SENCOs and school leaders is geographically broad, it is opportunistic in nature, which means there are significant barriers to generalising from the individual testimonials. However, the point of this book is not to generalise, but to highlight the uniqueness and individuality of each SENCO and their role. Their insights may not be generalisable, but they are certainly a strong basis for learning from the experience of others.

The voice of children and young people themselves and their families is also of central importance, so the book concludes with three individual stories. Each story shines a light on the impact that the SENCO has had on the lives and outcomes of individual pupils. As is the case with the SENCOs and school leaders, the identities of any pupils have also been kept confidential. In some cases, contextual changes have been made or similar individual stories have been conflated to ensure a higher level of identity protection and to emphasise key points.

An interesting observation about SENCOs is that their work can sometimes go completely unnoticed when things are going well for learners. For example, some teachers are unaware of the full breadth of support that a SENCO can provide until they have a pupil with SEND in their class who needs something more than adaptive teaching. Other teachers discover the practical reality of the SENCO role when they are asked to take on the responsibility by the Headteacher. As one SENCO put it:

> I thought becoming the SENCO would be straightforward because I've seen others do the role at my school and it looks easy. They get more non-contact time to basically keep the SEN register up to date and sort out the interventions timetable. Well, that's what I thought, but I was so wrong! There is so much to do. . . . I'd just not realised the full extent of the role. I was evaluating the impact of interventions, speaking to all these external agencies and having endless meetings with parents. It is rewarding, but I just had no idea about all this other work going on in the background. Full kudos to all SENCOs.
>
> (Interviewed SENCO)

A similar set of misconceptions can be found within the parental community too. Parents may be aware of what SENCOs do if they or somebody they know has had reason to engage with SENCOs in the past. For example, if a friend's child had SEND, or if the parent themselves was a professional working in education or a related field. But for some parents, their first real insight into what a SENCO does may well be when they begin to have conversations with them about the needs of their own child. At this point, the SENCO transforms from being a role they may never have heard about to being a central figure in their child's provision and arguably their child's life.

For SENCOs and others reading this book, it should be understood from the outset that its purpose is broad and multifaceted. Different readers are likely to draw upon different elements that are most relevant to them. For some readers, this book will provide strategies for inclusion that can be used to change the culture and ethos of a school over time. For other readers, the book will share effective practice on adaptive teaching as well as practical ideas that support coproduction and inclusion.

If reading the book as a whole, it may come across as sporadic as the substance and style varies between chapters and even within chapters. In part, this is a reflection of the complex and diverse nature of the SENCO role. However, what binds all of the chapters together is the desire to share the truth about who SENCOs are and the work they do. This will help to ensure that others can learn from these experiences and that SENCOs can finally get the recognition they deserve.

Whilst the core audience for this book is current or aspiring SENCOs, it is written in such a way that it should also be valuable to school leaders and to classroom teachers, whether they are in mainstream or specialist settings. The book is designed to include strategic perspectives, but it also includes plenty of practical advice and guidance. The aim was for readers to be able to implement immediate changes to their practice that support ever-greater inclusion in our schools. If every reader makes just one change, the cumulative impact will be substantial.

## A Note on Terminology

There are a lot of acronyms in education, and this is particularly true when it comes to SEND. Therefore, a glossary is provided at the back of the book to help you as the reader should you come across an acronym you have not seen before. The acronyms SEN and SEND are generally used interchangeably.

When it comes to discussing children and young people with SEND, several terms are used interchangeably throughout the book. For example, 'children' is sometimes written by itself, but this may well include 'young people' as well. Similarly, the terms 'pupils' and 'learners' are used frequently to refer to 'children and young people'.

When discussing the parents and/or carers of pupils with SEND, again multiple terms are used interchangeably, and this typically reflects the preference of the author or of the individual being quoted. For example, the following terms are used: 'parents/carers', 'parent carers' or 'families'. Where the term 'parents' is used in isolation, this can be assumed to also include carers.

The authors gave a great deal of thought as to whether identity-first language should be used for specific needs. For example, should we say 'a dyslexic child' or 'a child with dyslexia'? Our experience tells us that some people prefer the former as they would argue that dyslexia is part of who they are. However, other people prefer the latter as they feel they are a person first and foremost and do not wish to be defined by their SEN. This also varies by need. For example, describing somebody as 'an autistic child' is likely to be more socially acceptable than describing somebody as 'a disabled child'. For consistency, the authors have typically used the approach of saying 'a child with SEND' rather than 'a SEND child', but we recognise this preference will not work for all individuals and all needs.

## Introducing the Authors

The authors of this book are Adam Boddison and Maxine O'Neill. Whilst both authors have a significant professional experience of working in the SEND sector, their professional journeys and areas of expertise are quite different. In combining their respective perspectives, Adam and Maxine are able to provide a rich set of insights across a broad range of topics that are relevant for inclusion. They do not agree on everything, which may become apparent as readers progress through the various chapters. However, what unites Adam and Maxine is their fundamental belief that there is still much more to be done to create an education system that is truly inclusive.

Adam's professional experience has generally been in mainstream schools, policy and governance; whilst Maxine's professional experience has generally been in special schools, safeguarding and school leadership. As a consequence, their combined experience brings both breadth and depth.

On a personal level, it should be acknowledged that Adam and Maxine are brother and sister. They grew up together and therefore have similar values and perspectives of the world. Despite having both been involved with SEND for several years, this is the first time they have worked together formally. Hopefully, it will not be the last.

### *Professor Adam Boddison OBE*

Adam trained to be a secondary mathematics teacher in 2004, and he went on to teach in multiple primary and secondary schools over the following eight years. It is fair to say that Adam's work as a mathematics teacher was not typical. In addition to teaching pupils in the classroom, he ran a 'maths roadshow' and supported groups of parents to be more confident in their own mathematics abilities. The organisation that was then known as the Specialist Schools and Academies Trust appointed Adam as a *Lead Practitioner for Mathematics*, which saw him innovating on the development of classroom resources and championing the subject at both regional and national levels. He later went on to be Lead Editor for a series of A-level mathematics textbooks aligned to the Cambridge International Education syllabus and published by Harper Collins.

Alongside his teaching, Adam was actively engaged with education research, and he published a PhD on the use of video conferencing for teaching maths to gifted 10-year-olds. At the time, video conferencing was frowned upon in schools due to safeguarding concerns with many believing that the technology was unnecessary. This was of course 15 years before the global pandemic, during which video conferencing played a major part in providing continued education to hundreds of thousands of children. Adam's research explored online pedagogy and tactics for remote behaviour management. During this period Adam also qualified as a clinical hypnotherapist and ran a practice that focused on supporting children to tackle anxiety and phobias.

For over a decade, Adam held multiple roles at the University of Warwick. For example, Adam worked in the Warwick Maths Institute supporting A-level students to access Further Mathematics. He published a book for teachers called *The Maths Behind The Magic*, which brought together his passion for magic tricks with his passion for mathematics, and he delivered maths inspiration talks around the country, such as *Maths in the Movies*. Adam's other roles at the university included working on summer schools, fundraising for scholarships and a decade providing pastoral care for students living in university accommodation. Adam's final role at the University of Warwick was as the Director of the Centre for Professional Education, where his remit spanned international education business development and teacher education across the early years, primary and secondary phases.

In 2015, Adam was appointed as the Chief Executive Officer for nasen (the National Association for Special Educational Needs). During his six-year tenure, nasen's business model was revised, including making membership free of charge, which saw a ten-fold increase in membership numbers from fewer than 4000 to more than 40,000. Adam's successor has further grown this to more than 100,000 members. Adam was a key player in the creation of Whole School SEND, a consortium of charities and other organisations supporting the SEND community. He later became Chair of Whole School SEND and was Founding Chair of the National SEND Reference Group, which was established in partnership with the Department for Education.

Highlights of Adam's time at nasen include launching the first annual nasen Awards, which shines a light on effective practice and incredible people across the entire SEND community. He also led an independent review of SEND for the Bailiwick of Guernsey, and he has conducted multiple independent reviews of SEND in schools.

Adam has remained actively involved in SEND and in education more broadly through his research and writing and his Visiting Professor role at the University of Wolverhampton. He has been actively involved with school governance, including being Chair of Governors at a primary school and a further education college. He was also a Trustee for three different Multi-Academy Trusts spanning primary, secondary and special schools. In 2022, Adam was awarded the OBE for services to children and young people with SEND.

Currently, Adam is Visiting Professor at the University of Leicester School of Business and at Stranmillis University College. He is also the Chief Executive Officer at the Association for Project Management, which is a multidisciplinary professional body with a royal charter that facilitates the delivery of societal benefit across the public, private and third sectors.

## Maxine O'Neill

Maxine trained to be a primary teacher in 2006, opting for the four-year in-depth route to qualified teacher status. Alongside her studies, Maxine was already active in the field of professional development where she was delivering training courses for foster carers across a range of areas, including early childhood development, trauma-informed practice and responding to challenging behaviours.

Having completed her studies, Maxine's first teaching position was at an education and behavioural difficulties (EBD) setting called Hope School in Liverpool that provides for children in key stages one to three. Within four years, Maxine had completed the National Award in SEN Coordination, and she was appointed as the SENCO at the school. At the same time, the Children and Families Act 2014 was enacted, and a new SEND Code of Practice 2015 was introduced, bringing in a national set of SEND reforms. These reforms changed EBD schools to SEMH schools, prompting a renewed focus on understanding underlying needs rather than purely seeking to minimise unwanted behaviours. This is when Maxine began her journey into psychological practices.

Maxine's career continued to develop at pace at Hope School, where she moved from SENCO to Assistant Headteacher to Deputy Headteacher to Headteacher. She also completed five years in a designated safeguarding role. During Maxine's tenure, the school was twice graded outstanding by Ofsted with recognition in multiple years at the Pearson National Teaching Awards.

Maxine has continued to share her SEMH expertise beyond her school. This includes her active engagement with the Attachment Research Community (ARC). Maxine, along with members of ARC, set up Hope School as the first ARC Learning Hub. Maxine went on to work with the virtual school as a founding member to develop the HEARTs project. The HEARTs project is an attachment- and trauma-informed network of schools in Liverpool who work towards a framework to become more responsive to behaviours. The HEARTs project was recognised with an 'Impact Through Partnership' award in the Pearson National Teaching Awards in 2023.

Maxine has also coproduced conferences with the Child and Adolescent Mental Health Service (CAMHS) for schools focusing on trauma-informed strategies in the primary classroom.

Maxine also took on a role as SEMH Advisor for Liverpool Local Authority around a whole school response to behaviour as part of the SEND sufficiency plan. More recently Maxine has supported a number of enhanced provisions to set up across the city working on curriculum content and staff CPD.

Maxine is a visiting lecturer at Liverpool Hope University, Edge Hill University and Manchester Metropolitan University, where she provides insights into attachment and trauma, neurodiversity, the inclusive classroom, the PACE approach and behaviour management, to name a few. In addition, Maxine is a qualified Theraplay practitioner with Theraplay UK, who has worked to implement a therapeutic holistic approach in all the work she does.

Outside of school, Maxine is a foster carer, an active member of the local netball league, attends Family Martial Arts and regularly attends the gym around spending time with her family and friends. She is an advocate for a strong work-life balance and having a healthy body and mind.

# 1 Evolution of the SENCO Role

The SENCO role is of critical importance in schools. As if to underline this point, it is only the role of the Headteacher and the SENCO that are described in statute and compulsorily required in maintained schools in England (Tutt, 2016b; Yates and Boddison, 2020, p. 29; Curran et al., 2018, p. 3). Of these two roles, only the SENCO is required to be a qualified teacher. Further still, the SENCO must also attain the Masters level qualification, the National Award in SEN Coordination, although this requirement will soon be replaced by the need to attain the leadership level SENCO National Professional Qualification (NPQ) (HM Government, 2022, p. 44).

This chapter will provide some commentary on the evolution of the SENCO role over time. In addition to exploring some of the statutory expectations of the SENCO role, there will be a discussion on the additional expectations that are placed on SENCOs by their colleagues, by learners, by families and by SENCOs themselves. The intention is to expose and explore the aspects of the SENCO role that many people are unaware of and to provide a peek behind the curtain into the secret lives of SENCOs.

## What Do We Mean by 'the SENCO'?

Asking what we mean by 'the SENCO' might sound like an unnecessary question given its prominence in statutory guidance and the expectations set out in multiple SEN Codes of Practice (DfE, 1994; DfES, 2001; DfE and DoH, 2015). However, the reality is that the SENCO role varies significantly from school to school as do individual perceptions of the purpose of the role.

The National Association for Special Educational Needs (nasen) helpfully has a page on its website that sets out what a SENCO is:

> SENCOs, who must be a qualified teacher in mainstream schools, oversee the strategic development of SEN policy and provision and as such is advised to form part of the leadership team. In addition, they ensure the implementation of the SEN policy on a day-to-day basis.
>
> They are a key point of contact for colleagues and can offer support and advice for the identification of needs and suitable provision to meet those needs. Through provision management they will maintain an overview of the progress of pupils with SEND and will seek to develop practice to ensure the effectiveness of interventions and support.
>
> (nasen, no date)

From this brief description, it is easy to see how different interpretations about the purpose and implementation of the role can arise. For the purposes of this chapter, the authors are largely referring to the role of SENCO as it would typically exist in a state-funded, primary, secondary or special school. However, it is acknowledged that many other models and approaches exist depending upon the specific contexts. For example, some schools 'buy in' a SENCO who may offer the same service to multiple schools. Some schools have a Trust SENCO, which may either be instead of or in addition to SENCOs in each of the individual schools in the Trust. Some schools have the Headteacher fulfilling the SENCO role, and in others it is seen as purely administrative. This book has sought to draw on examples from a wide range of contexts and approaches to ensure it has broad applicability and relevance.

Unlike mainstream schools, the statutory guidance does not require special schools to have a SENCO (DfE and DoH, 2015, p. 92). However, there are plenty of examples of special schools that choose to have SENCOs, and these are typically part of the senior leadership team (Richards et al., 2023, p. 81). In some special schools, the SENCO essentially undertakes the

DOI: 10.4324/9781032634807-1

administrative duties relating to EHC plans, such as organising annual reviews, monitoring funding and commissioning services. But in other special schools, the SENCO leads on interventions or is responsible for the deployment of resources for universal and targeted provision. In some special schools, the Headteacher is seen as the SENCO, or there may be no SENCO at all. To help provide clarity between the role of a SENCO in a special school and the role of Headteacher, a RACI matrix can be helpful, and this concept is discussed in Chapter 2.

The Headteacher at one special school described how they see all of their teachers as SENCOs, given that all of their pupils have EHC plans. There are some who would extend this further to argue that all teachers in mainstream schools are SENCOs (Harris, 2019). Given the arguments already made about the critical importance of the SENCO role, there is a risk that this type of approach undermines the professional status of SENCOs. The role of a SENCO and a teacher of SEN are different, and conflating them is 'flippant and risks trivialising the [SENCO] role, which is already poorly understood by many teachers' (Ross, 2019).

## The Evolution of the SENCO Role

Pre-pandemic, the educational landscape was described as one 'where school funding is deemed by many to be insufficient, where both the number of pupils with SEND and complexity of their needs is increasing, and where both the recruitment and retention of teachers are challenging' (Boddison, 2019b). This challenging operating environment is arguably more acute now than it was then, and it has undeniably exacerbated long-standing pressures on SENCOs.

In considering the evolution of the SENCO role, a sensible starting point is the Warnock Report (1978), since this is where the terminology of SEN derives, somewhat progressing beyond the previously used terms of 'learning disability' or 'impairment'. It was 16 years after the Warnock report before the SENCO role was formally introduced by the 1994 SEN Code of Practice (DfE, 1994), which followed the 1993 Education Act (HMSO, 1993). SENCOs did exist in schools prior to 1994, but this was the school's choice rather than it being a statutory requirement. It was the 1994 SEN Code of Practice that first compelled schools to appoint SENCOs, and the role has been a statutory requirement ever since (Curran, 2019c, p. 6).

The first SEN Code of Practice identified seven key responsibilities for the SENCO (DfE, 1994, pp. 20–21):

- The day-to-day operation of the school's SEN policy
- Liaising and advising with fellow teachers
- Coordinating provision for children with special educational needs
- Maintaining the school's SEN register and overseeing the records on all pupils with special educational needs
- Liaising with parents of children with special educational needs
- Contributing to the in-service training of staff
- Liaising with external agencies including the educational psychology service and career support agencies, medical and social services and voluntary bodies

It is notable that even this initial SEN Code of Practice with its relatively few responsibilities reflected the breadth and complexity of the SENCO role. Both educational and pastoral responsibilities were included alongside a significant portfolio of stakeholders.

Most of the listed responsibilities are operational since they are either about liaison or they are administrative in nature. Over time, successive iterations of legislation and statutory guidance have demanded that the SENCO role be more strategic (Packer, 2014, p. 1). For example, the Teacher Training Agency (TTA) published National Standards for SENCOs (TTA, 1998), which elevated the role beyond tactical and towards leadership. These standards used terminology such as 'strategic direction', 'development' and 'leading and managing' to describe the expectations of SENCOs, positioning SENCOs as central to 'the development and progression of inclusion within schools' (Brewin and Knowler, 2023, p. 11). The intention was that the SENCO, in a more strategic role, could drive a 'whole school approach' to SEND provision (Layton, 2005).

Despite the best intentions of policy makers in 1998, many SENCOs did not become sufficiently strategic in response to the National Standards, with administrative tasks still accounting for the majority of SENCOs' allocated time for many years to come (Curran and Boddison, 2021).

There was an attempt to address this in the 2001 SEN Code of Practice by stating that 'settings may find it effective for the SENCO to be a member of the senior management team' (DfES, 2001, p. 35). However, the failure to stipulate that the SENCO should be a qualified teacher resulted in the sustained common practice of schools appointing teaching assistants or administrative staff to the SENCO role. It was a further seven years before the requirement for the SENCO to be a qualified teacher was introduced via the SENCO Regulations (HM Government, 2008).

The SENCO role has continued to evolve both in its own right and in response to wider changes in education policy to the point where it is now embedded as a standard role in schools in England (Richards et al., 2023, p. 74). Despite the SENCO becoming a pivotal role in schools (Beere, 2014), there are still some that do not appear to be taking the statutory requirements seriously enough. For example, there are some schools that have appointed the Headteacher as the SENCO, but the Headteacher has then delegated all of the responsibilities of the role to a teaching assistant or an administrator, both of whom are unqualified teachers. In such situations, the Headteacher is the SENCO in name only, and such approaches represent a clear attempt to 'game the system'.

Appointing an appropriate person into the SENCO role is important because the right person can be an enabler of inclusive practice rather than inadvertently inhibiting it. Suppose the Headteacher is appointed into the role of SENCO and that they do not intend to game the system but to fulfil their SENCO duties sincerely. The question then arises as to how easy this is to achieve in practice and whether or not Headteachers inherently have a conflict of interest if they are also the named SENCO. For example, if the SENCO makes a decision on SEND provision that parents and carers disagree with, then there is limited scope for internal escalation without resorting to governors. This is problematic as governors ought to be strategic and not routinely operational (Boddison, 2021, p. 49).

Additionally, the SENCO might typically lobby the Headteacher on resource allocation decisions related to SEND. If the Headteacher and the SENCO are the same person, does such advocacy disappear? Similarly, who challenges the Headteacher on matters where pupils with SEND are being sanctioned or excluded if the SENCO is the Headteacher? Of course, the priorities of the Headteacher and the SENCO in a school ought to be fully aligned. However, the reality is that working in an education system with depleted resources and accountability measures that are skewed towards academic outcomes over inclusion means this is sadly not always the case.

## The Current Iteration of the SENCO Role

It is challenging to make genuine and meaningful observations about the current iteration of the SENCO role because it varies so much between schools and because it is so contextual in nature (Hallet and Hallet, 2010, p. 1; Knowler et al., 2023, p. 1; Curran, 2019c, p. 6). Within a school, the SENCO role is different to every other role, and specific skills are needed to be effective (Fitzgerald and Radford, 2022). The absence of both internal and external comparators means the SENCO role has become 'confused and contested' (Curran, 2019a), making it difficult for SENCOs to assess whether they are under or over delivering as expectations are unclear. In too many instances, Headteachers and SENCOs themselves lack clarity on the precise scope of the SENCO role (Sobel, 2018, p. 50).

Extending this theme of uniqueness further, Kearns (2005) makes the point that it is difficult to define a single coherent identity for all SENCOs because each of them can have a role that is made up of multiple other inter-related roles. Further still, attempting to pre-determine the parameters of the SENCO role is likely to be undesirable (Huthwaite and Howieson, 2023, p. 49) as there is no one approach that will work to include all children in a school.

When discussing the value of 'a culture a trust, agency and inclusion', the CEO of the Chartered College of Teaching, Dame Alison Peacock, provides a good example of the uniqueness of the SENCO role. She emphasises the importance of 'building a deep understanding [of children with SEND] in partnership with family members and other agencies' (Peacock, 2018, p. 40). On the one hand, such uniqueness is powerful, since it provides the scope to deliver bespoke personalised learning experiences for pupils. But on the other hand, there is a risk that the SENCO ends up being perceived as a hero (Oldham and Radford, 2011) who can solve all problems for all children with SEND. Given the existing workload and retention issues within the teaching profession, which have been amplified by the global pandemic (Boddison and Curran, 2022; Johnson and Coleman, 2023), placing this type of expectation on one individual seems unwise.

## SENCO Responsibilities

Despite the overarching uniqueness of the SENCO role, there are core activities that are common to most SENCOs in most schools. The most recent iteration of the SEND Code of Practice (DfE and DoH, 2015, pp. 108–109) is statutory guidance that lists the following as responsibilities of the SENCO:

- Overseeing the day-to-day operation of the school's SEN policy
- Co-ordinating provision for children with SEN
- Liaising with the relevant Designated Teacher where a looked-after pupil has SEN
- Advising on the graduated approach to providing SEN support
- Advising on the deployment of the school's delegated budget and other resources to meet pupils' needs effectively
- Liaising with parents of pupils with SEN
- Liaising with early years providers, other schools, educational psychologists, health and social care professionals, and independent or voluntary bodies
- Being a key point of contact with external agencies, especially the local authority and its support services
- Liaising with potential next providers of education to ensure a pupil and their parents are informed about options and a smooth transition is planned
- Working with the headteacher and school governors to ensure that the school meets its responsibilities under the Equality Act (2010) with regard to reasonable adjustments and access arrangements
- Ensuring that the school keeps the records of all pupils with SEN up to date

Comparing the eleven responsibilities in the 2015 SEND Code of Practice with the seven responsibilities in the 1994 SEN Code of Practice, we can make several observations. Firstly, there are now more responsibilities for SENCOs, and they are more complex, meaning that SENCOs now have more to do. Secondly, although the 2015 SEND Code of Practice, considered in its entirety, contains a clear amplification of the strategic nature of the SENCO role, this is not sufficiently explicit in the listed key responsibilities of the SENCO. It would seem that in an effort to avoid prescribing a single, specific approach to schools, policy makers have inadvertently signalled that it is optional rather than optimum for the SENCO to undertake a strategic role in the school.

There are other lists of SENCO responsibilities too, including Curran's set of 24 responsibilities, which is described as 'not exhaustive' (2019c, pp. 15–17). Curran's list is arguably more extensive and more strategic than the responsibilities listed in the 2015 SEND Code of Practice, since it includes duties such as the following:

- Monitoring the effectiveness of the additional support in place
- Conducting data analysis to identify needs, requirements for provision, progress of pupils, specific groups or trends, which may indicate a need for short or more longer-term support
- Reviewing the strategic development of SEN across the school, including identifying any areas for development, for example parental participation

## SENCO Workload and Administration

Curran's list also identifies 'paperwork' as a key responsibility for SENCOs, echoing concerns from other studies that administrative expectations are contributing to excessive workload (Curran et al., 2018; Boddison and Curran, 2022). It would be unfair to say that the administrative aspect of the SENCO role is solely down to statutory guidance as it can sometimes arise due to the expectations of Headteachers who see the role as administrative or due to excessive micro-management that demands yet more paperwork (Smith, 2022b).

More generally, there is broad agreement that the SENCO role has significant workload demands with an insufficient amount of protected time to deliver against expectations (Curran et al., 2018; Packer, 2014, p. 16). Much like teaching itself, the job is never done as there is always something more that could be done. In many ways, excessive SENCO workload is a self-fulfilling prophecy as the more a SENCO does, the more they find there is to be done

(Packer, 2014, p. 139). From a strategic perspective, this underlines the need for building capability and capacity for SEND into the wider workforce, rather than relying solely on the SENCO for all things SEND. The most inclusive schools are those where SEND is a whole school priority and is everybody's responsibility.

---

### Box 1.1 Why do teachers choose to become a SENCO?

Given that the role of the SENCO is so misunderstood, under-resourced and under-respected (Gedge and Phillips, 2019, p. 51), it is reasonable to ask why a teacher would choose to become a SENCO. As with many roles, both in education and beyond, being the SENCO was traditionally seen by many as a 'job for life', but it has subsequently become a potential route to school leadership given its increasingly strategic status. This highlights that career progression is one reason why a teacher may take on the SENCO role (Hellawell, 2017), not least because it gives them an opportunity to develop knowledge and skills that may be useful for school leadership (Dobson and Douglas, 2020).

Dobson and Douglas (2020) undertook a specific study to consider the question of why teachers become SENCOs, and they identified 'professional experience' was one such reason. In particular, they found that some SENCOs took on the role because they had a track record of being good with paperwork or because they have previously found it rewarding to work with children with SEND.

Some SENCOs can have ethical or social justice motivations for undertaking the role. For example, a SENCO might want to ensure that children they encounter in their professional life receive the same standard of education and opportunity as their own children. Dobson and Douglas (2020) describe such SENCOs as experiencing 'a sense of cathartic justice' through providing such advocacy. Another example of an ethical motivation would be SENCOs taking on the role because they feel they are the best person available to do it within the setting or because they have seen others do it poorly (Dobson and Douglas, 2020).

Whilst there are often laudable motivations for becoming a SENCO, this is not always the case. For example, one SENCO described that they did not want to become a SENCO, but they felt they had no option but to take on the role 'because there was nobody else who could do it'. Similarly, another SENCO reported that they never planned to do so, but they 'kind of fell into the role'. In this particular instance, the Headteacher wanted a senior member of staff to undertake the role and they were the chosen person.

In some schools, the SENCO role does not yet have the professional status it deserves, and this was evident from the accounts of several SENCOs. For example, one SENCO reported how staff in her school were 'rotated in and out of the role'. The argument from the Headteacher was that they saw the SENCO responsibility as being similar to that of the 'gifted and talented coordinator', which was a dynamic responsibility allocated each year.

However, the SENCO was of the view that the real reason for taking this approach was to save money by 'gaming the system to avoid the requirement of having National SEN Coordination Award within three years of becoming the SENCO'. Another SENCO reported that in his school the SENCO role was typically allocated to an Early Career Teacher (ECT) and positioned as a 'development opportunity'. He went on to say that any challenge to this approach was countered with the fact that the SENCO was line managed by an Assistant Headteacher with responsibility for inclusion as part of her remit.

Whilst it did not arise explicitly through the interviews with SENCOs and school leaders, a question to consider is whether some SENCOs might take on the role because it leads to more time out of the classroom. Given the increasing accountability pressures on teachers to deliver outstanding progress and attainment data for their pupils, might a full-time SENCO role be a good place to avoid unwanted scrutiny? That is not to say that an individual acting for such reasons is necessarily a poor teacher, but rather that they do not enjoy the typical monitoring and oversight that comes with contemporary classroom teaching.

On the theme of underperforming teachers, one Headteacher did share an honest reflection that they had once promoted a teacher into the SENCO role 'because it was easier and cheaper than moving them on'. She went on to defend her decision, arguing that this was the quickest way to get this teacher out of the classroom and get a more effective teacher into the classroom. When asked whether she thought she had done right by pupils with

SEND, she said, 'The best thing I can do as a Headteacher for pupils with SEND is to give them access to the best teacher I can'. On the matter of the newly promoted SENCO, the Headteacher said she recognised there was still a performance issue to deal with, but that it was easier for her to monitor and manage the person as a SENCO outside the classroom than as a teacher inside the classroom. This is an interesting insight as it challenges the notion that there is consistently less scrutiny for non-teaching SENCOs than there is for classroom teachers.

As we can see, there is no single and clear motivation for a teacher to become a SENCO, and the decision might not always be driven by the teacher themselves. The reality is that those who choose to be a SENCO are likely to be considering a range of 'personal, organisational and social factors' to help them with this important choice (Dobson and Douglas, 2020).

## Reflection Questions

1. In what ways is becoming a SENCO good for your career?
2. What are the benefits and drawbacks of having a SENCO who still has a regular classroom teaching commitment?

## *SENCOs as Strategic Leaders*

A long-standing debate is whether or not SENCOs need to be on the senior leadership team in a school in order to be strategic. The current SEND Code of Practice states that SENCOs will be most effective if they are part of the school leadership team (DfE and DoH, 2015, p. 108), but it stops short of mandating this. Similarly, the Code's use of the expression 'school leadership team' rather than 'senior leadership team' has further broadened the scope for multiple interpretations with school leaders able to claim that appointing the SENCO to a middle leadership position is aligned to policy expectations. In any case, Clarke and Done (2021) are clear that having a SENCO within the school's leadership is vital for a whole school approach to inclusion.

The extent to which the leadership aspects of the SENCO role are expected or carried out varies widely between schools (Tissot, 2013). Furthermore, there are some scenarios in which the SENCO's role as a leader is uncertain or deliberately limiting. For example, several SENCOs described that they were part of the senior leadership team, but in practice this meant that they were only invited to leadership team meetings for particular agenda items deemed as relevant to SEND and not for the whole meeting. This was seen as problematic because it meant that SENCOs were less empowered to drive a whole school approach to inclusion. One SENCO described this as her being 'a member of the leadership team in name only' and that 'it said a lot about the prioritisation and importance of SEND to leaders in that school'.

Conversely, there were SENCOs who described the same limiting approach to their role on the senior leadership team but saw this as a positive tactic. Given the workload pressures on SENCOs, they felt the additional expectations of being a 'fully-fledged member of the senior leadership team' would be too much. For example, they argued it was good to remove additional tasks such as being 'on-call', doing 'bus duty' and having 'excessive line management responsibilities' that they felt were far removed from their role as a SENCO.

The broader notion of leadership in a school setting can be interpreted in different ways, and it can be informal, such as mentoring (Middleton and Kay, 2020, p. 86), which can provide additional uncertainty for SENCOs about the parameters of their role. Ultimately, irrespective of whether the SENCO is a fully embedded member of the senior leadership team and irrespective of whether the role is formal or informal, the underlying principle is that the SENCO must have an appropriate mechanism to have strategic influence. This is essential since SEND does not exist in a vacuum. Every aspect of school provision and every strategic decision that is made could help or hinder a school's ambition for inclusion.

This discussion about the current iteration of the SENCO role has now come full circle to the debate about the balance of strategic and operational responsibilities. As discussed earlier in the chapter, the SENCO role has become more strategic over time in line with statutory guidance. However, irrespective of what the legislation stipulates, the extent to which the SENCO role is strategic varies from school to school. In one school, the SENCO is part of the senior leadership team and highly strategic, but in another school they are essentially a glorified administrator, and everything in between. Indeed, it can often be hard to determine where on this spectrum a particular SENCO role lies as it does not always remain consistent. Curran (2019c, p. 19) discusses whether a SENCO is a person who advises or a person who acts, which could be a useful mechanism for measuring where about on the strategic-operational spectrum a particular SENCO is operating.

Despite the ongoing debate, Tutt (2016a, p. 13) is clear that the intent of the Children and Families Act (Gov UK, 2014) and the SEND Code of Practice (DfE and DoH, 2015) is for the SENCO role to be strategic. Tutt goes on to emphasise the importance of every teacher being a teacher of pupils with SEND, redistributing some of the operational expectations that had previously sat unsustainably with SENCOs alone.

---

### Box 1.2  The challenge of squeezed school budgets

The Institute for Fiscal Studies (IFS, 2023) makes the point that although the government has chosen to increase school spending in England at recent spending reviews, there has effectively been a funding squeeze since 2010. More recently, real terms funding for schools has risen by 10% (£5bn) between 2019/20 and 2023/24, but rampant inflationary pressures mean this increase has been insufficient (IFS, 2023).

Within schools, staffing is often the most significant expense, and this might typically represent 80% of a school's budget (TES, 2022; The Key, 2022). This proportion is arguably more acute still for special schools or for mainstream schools with a higher prevalence of SEND, since the staff–pupil ratio will be higher.

When school budgets are squeezed due to the external operating environment, Headteachers will clearly look at all options, but often it will be staffing where cuts need to be made. In a situation where it is deemed unsafe to reduce staffing levels but this is the only affordable option, what can Headteachers do? What should Headteachers do?

### Reflection Questions

1. How can schools be more financially efficiently without reducing staffing levels?
2. How might technology bring greater flexibility for schools of the future? How might this impact the overall cost of running a school?

---

## *Phase-Specific SENCO Variations*

There is a long-established adage that primary school teachers are teachers of children, whilst secondary school teachers are teachers of subjects (Grauer, 1995, p. 147). If we accept that there is some truth in this adage, then it stands to reason that this contrast should be echoed in differences in SENCO roles across the primary and secondary phases.

The increased scale and complexity of secondary schools in comparison to most primary schools arguably provides a more challenging context for SENCOs due to the greater number of teachers and support staff they have to liaise with and support (Fitzgerald and Radford, 2022). Similarly, secondary school SENCOs are more likely to have a deputy SENCO or administrative support (Curran et al., 2021) or to be line managing a large team of teaching assistants (Richards et al., 2023, p. 77), making it more of a leadership role by default.

Conversely, it could be argued that the larger teams in the secondary phase constitute a greater set of available resources. In practice, this could make the role easier because the responsibilities for SEND are more distributed, whereas in primary schools such responsibilities are likely to rest more firmly with the SENCO. Similarly, SENCOs in the primary phase often have less time than those in the secondary phase, with the most common amount of time allocated for primary and secondary SENCOs being 0.5 to 1 day and 3 to 3.5 days respectively (Curran et al., 2018, p. 16).

Another phase-specific observation is that, unlike primary schools, it is common for secondary schools to appoint Deputy Headteachers with responsibility either for pastoral provision or for teaching and learning. Unless the SENCO is directly line managed by the Headteacher, this means that the SENCO role is likely to be positioned as either pastoral or within teaching and learning. Whichever way the SENCO role is positioned, this might inadvertently indicate the Headteacher's perception and expectations of the role. Interestingly, this calls into question the debate about whether or not the SENCO should be on the senior leadership team and instead suggests that the more important question is about who they report to and how this shapes their strategic influence.

### SENCOs as Pastoral Leaders or Drivers of Quality-First Teaching

There remains a lack of clarity as to whether the SENCO is a pastoral role or a teaching and learning role. The truth is that it spans both, which is why it is such a powerful pathway to Headship. Many pathways to Headship are either via the pastoral route or the teaching and learning route, but the SENCO role provides both, once again demonstrating the breadth, complexity and centrality of the role.

From a teaching and learning perspective, SENCOs in all types of schools are well placed to influence the development of the curriculum to ensure it is personalised (Richards et al., 2023, p. 81). In addition to this, SENCOs should be conducting regular learning walks (Taylor, 2018, pp. 98–99) to ensure provision across the school is inclusive. It is easy to make the case that the pedagogical aspect of the SENCO role is one of the hardest teaching and learning responsibilities that exists within a school, not least because their focus is on those pupils with the most complex needs (Rozsahegyi and Lambert, 2023, p. 36). Returning to the cross-functional nature of the SENCO role, it can be argued that seeking to close the attainment gap between pupils with SEND and other pupils is impossible if SEND and attainment are managed separately (Sobel, 2018, p. 83).

The disproportionate number of pupils with SEND who are excluded or who use behaviour to communicate their needs means that SENCOs are often tasked with pastoral responsibilities alongside any teaching and learning responsibilities. Such pastoral responsibilities can extend more widely into families, particularly where they may also have SEND or they may blame themselves for their children's SEND or for not identifying it sooner (Francis, 2012; Hewitt and Tarrant, 2015, p. 142). This form of self-blame and guilt is too often due to being overly self-critical.

The skillset that SENCOs need to work with SEND in families is important too and often overlooked. For example, there are some needs where the use of touch is therapeutic and useful for the child's development. However, if the cultural norms in the home do not lend themselves easily to the use of touch, it is often SENCOs who are working with families to develop this alongside any provision they have put into place at the school. This is all part of meaningful coproduction, working with families as equal partners, since the insights about cultural norms at home are also of huge value in shaping provision in school.

### SENCO Ethics

Returning to the complexity of the SENCO role, another aspect that can too often go unnoticed are the constant ethical decisions that SENCOs have to make. For those SENCOs in leadership positions, the need for strong ethical leadership becomes even more essential (Morewood, 2018). In relation to most (perhaps all with the possible exception of the DSL?) other roles in a school, the SENCO has to deal with a greater volume and complexity of ethical issues.

At a fundamental level, one the regular judgements that a SENCO must make is whether or not to include a pupil on the school's SEN register. On the face of it, this might appear to be an administrative matter, but the underlying principles could have far-reaching and unintended consequences. That is because this decision is really about determining whether or not it is in the best interests of a child to label them as having SEND.

One of the arguments in favour of labelling is that it helps teachers to quickly understand the nature of the needs, and this means they are better placed to put effective provision in place at pace (Hewitt and Tarrant, 2015, p. 142). Hewitt and Tarrant do caveat this with the valid point that the child should not be defined by the label, but this is arguably not happening sufficiently well in practice. Labelling can also provide greater access to resources as well as providing children with a social identity (Norwich, 2013, p. 43).

The alternative approach to labelling is to really know and understand the child, including their strengths, their needs and their areas for development. As we saw earlier in this chapter, this approach is perhaps easier to achieve in a primary school setting where pupils typically spend most of their time with one or two teachers, unlike a secondary school where pupils may only spend a few hours a week at best with individual teachers. The labelling debate is not a new issue, and as far back as the 1970s, there were child-centred advocates arguing that we should 'label jars, not people' (Biklen et al., 1979, p. 3). One of the unintended consequences of labelling is that it can create stigma (Gross, 2023) or result in people being treated differently due to society's misconceptions, further exacerbating their needs or disabilities (Harpur, 2012, p. 326).

Whilst there are arguments for both the affordances and constraints of labelling, it is ultimately the SENCO who has to make this judgement call day in and day out, and it is pupils who then have to live with the potential life-changing consequences of these decisions. The current momentum on this debate is to move away from labelling as the drawbacks are deemed to outweigh the advantages (Gross, 2023; Algraigray and Boyle, 2017).

The culture of the school will also be a significant factor in the approach to identifying and recording SEND. Whilst one school might use categories of SEND (labels) as a mechanism for securing additional funding and resources, another school might use them to stereotype children or as a mechanism for limiting the level of accountability. For example, some school leaders present 'shadow data', which shows levels of progress and attainment for groups of children where those with SEND have been removed. Therefore, an unscrupulous leader might deliberately use an increased identification of SEND (more labels) to manipulate data for which they are accountable. This begs the politically charged question as to what the purpose of schools is all about and whether judgements on school effectiveness should be so heavily skewed towards progress and attainment data. As Norwich (2013, p. 163) puts it, are schools about pupils 'learning in a knowledge-centred curriculum', or are they about pupils 'participating in a society-centred curriculum'?

---

## Box 1.3  To label or not to label?

The definition of SEND is norm-referenced rather than criterion-referenced, which means the decision about whether or not a pupil has SEND is relative. It is dependent on both the needs of other pupils of the same age and the level of ordinarily available provision at the school. In practice, this means that for two children with exactly the same needs but attending different schools one might be deemed to have SEND and the other might not.

Let us consider the case of Chloe and Joanna, who attend different primary schools but have very similar profiles of need. Chloe's school has invested heavily in ensuring they are inclusive, and as such, there is a high level of ordinarily available provision. Chloe does not need to be put onto the SEND register because her needs can be met through quality-first teaching (sometimes referred to as 'high-quality teaching') and the school's standard offer.

Joanna is less fortunate. Her school has significant resource challenges, and their level of ordinarily available provision is much lower than in Chloe's school. However, Joanna has been identified as requiring provision that is 'additional to or different from' other children, so she has been included on the SEND register and receives additional support.

Both of these primary schools are feeder schools for the local secondary school, but when Chloe and Joanna transition from primary to secondary, something unexpected happens. The SENCO from the secondary school sees that Joanna has been identified as having SEND, and there is an enhanced transition put in place for her. Joanna is placed on the school's 'watch list' to see whether she needs to be on the SEND register at the secondary school.

However, Chloe's needs are not explicitly discussed as part of transition because she is not identified as having SEND. When Chloe reaches year eight, she is identified as having possible SEND as she is not making expected progress. She is eventually included on the SEND register in year nine, having missed out on two years of possible provision and support. The progress and attainment gaps between Chloe and her peers have widened, and other issues have started to emerge in relation to attendance, behaviour and self-esteem. For Chloe, this is the unintended consequence of effective inclusion in her previous setting.

In such a situation, the perception of the secondary school may well be that Chloe's primary school has failed to identify her needs, when the truth is that they were meeting those needs through their ordinarily available provision. Conversely, the perception of Joanna's school might well be that they were better at identifying and meeting needs, despite them having a lower level of ordinarily available provision. Such perceptions are easily adopted by local families with the consequence that Chloe's school becomes known locally as a school that does not identify SEND, despite its commitment to whole-school inclusion.

The purpose of this scenario is not to discourage school's from being inclusive, but rather to illustrate that effective inclusion can often be invisible.

> We also need to accept that having high aspirations, zero stigma and maximum inclusion often means making your support of children with SEND hard to pinpoint.

> The sooner all policy documents align on this message, the sooner we can achieve inclusion that feels not like an add-on, but as something integral, embedded and as such often invisible; something hidden at the whole-class level.
>
> *(Aubin, 2022)*

## Reflection Questions

1. What are your thoughts on the role of labels in articulating and communicating the needs of individual pupils?
2. What are the features of effective transition from primary school to secondary school for pupils with SEND?

The relativity of the definition of SEND means that SENCOs have to make subjective judgements about the complexity and severity of SEND that pupils have in order to determine whether or not they should be included on the SEND register (Wedell, 2019, p. 25). The experience and expertise of the SENCO will both be factors here, and such judgement calls add to the broader ethical dilemmas of labelling.

The discussion on identification has centred on the binary notion of whether or not a pupil has SEND, but the reality is of course more complex than this since SENCOs also need to determine the type of SEND and to recognise potential cooccurring needs. There is limited government guidance on the identification of types of SEND, and what does exist is not recent. For example, moderate learning difficulties (MLD) is interpreted in vastly different ways by different SENCOs (Lewis and Norwich, 2005, pp. 180–181). Similarly, SENCOs have to navigate and interpret broad concepts that are core to the SENCO role, such as 'inclusion' and 'behaviour' (Hewitt and Tarrant, 2015, p. 140), which will also elicit different understandings. This further emphasises the complexity and context-specific variability of the SENCO role.

## Box 1.4  Should the SENCO be a SEND expert?

SENCOs are often the go-to individual whenever there are questions about SEND. These questions could come from other teachers in the school, the Headteacher, governors, parents/carers or pupils themselves. This can be incredibly daunting for SENCOs as they are expected to be somewhat of an oracle on all things SEND. It could be argued that they are the SENCO so they should be knowledgeable on SEND, but is it reasonable to expect them to be a SEND expert?

It is certainly possible to have SEND expertise, but there should be a healthy degree of scepticism about anybody who claims to be a SEND expert. SEND is so broad, so deep and constantly evolving that it is impossible for any one person to know it all. SEND itself is made up of many different types of needs, from autism and dyslexia to SEMH and physical disabilities. These needs can also be, and often are, cooccurring, adding yet further complexity. Each of these areas of need are characterised by layers of knowledge, skills and understanding with many contested areas. For example, there is significant debate about the use of medication for children with ADHD (Scaglione, 2021; Sjostrom et al., 2023; Boland et al., 2020) and some who do not believe that dyslexia exists at all (Kirby, 2020). The SEND world is a world of worlds that cannot be completely grasped by one person alone.

Returning to the question about whether the SENCO should be a SEND expert, it makes sense for them to be the first point of contact for questions and queries, but they should not be expected to know everything. The requirement for SENCOs to have completed the National Award in SEN Coordination will provide at least a foundational knowledge of SEND for SENCOs to draw upon.

Given the complexity of SEND that children in a special school are likely to have, it is interesting that the SEND Code of Practice (DfE and DoH, 2015, p. 108) does not require SENCOs in special schools to have at least this foundational level of knowledge. It is surprising that the statutory minimum level of qualification to be a SENCO in a special school is lower than it is to be a SENCO in a mainstream school. Perhaps it is not seen as important for somebody to have the National Award in SEN Coordination in a special school if the formal role of the SENCO is not always required? Conversely, it is ultimately the class teacher who is responsible for the progress of all pupils in their class, including those with SEND. An effective approach uses the collaborative expertise of both teachers and the SENCO rather than relying on the individual expertise of one expert, whoever they may be. Such collaborative expertise plays a significant role shaping a school's ordinarily available provision and driving school improvement and inclusion priorities.

Shifting the focus of the question away from the SENCO, it is worth considering whether or not the Headteacher should be expected to be a SEND expert. The former Children's Minister Will Quince, who had policy responsibility for SEND, argued that Headteachers ought to have the National Award in SEN Coordination since 'inclusion starts from the top' (Booth, 2022).

There is certainly merit in the notion that Headteachers should have a thorough understanding of SEND and inclusion. As an example, consider the situation when the SENCO in a school makes the case to the Headteacher that they have put every possible measure in place to meet the needs of pupils with dyslexia. Without some knowledge and understanding of dyslexia and of inclusive practice more broadly, how can the Headteacher be assured that there is nothing more that could be done? In this situation, it can be very difficult for the Headteacher, or indeed the SEND Governor, to offer meaningful and targeted support and challenge to the SENCO.

One might argue that this is a matter of professional courtesy and trusting the SENCO as the school's SEND expert. But as has been argued, there is no such thing as a SEND expert. The rationale for providing challenge to a SENCO is not because they might intentionally seek to put a lesser provision in place, but because they too are continuously developing their competence and should not feel that they are on that journey alone.

An argument that is sometimes made is that Headteachers do not necessarily need to have SEND expertise as that is why they employ a SENCO, much like they do not necessarily need to have mathematics expertise in a secondary school as that is why they employ a Head of Mathematics. There is a semblance of logic to this argument, but SEND is fundamentally different to a curriculum area. For a start, the school is likely to have other mathematicians, and there is a good chance there will be a mathematician within the senior leadership team. In any event, all senior leaders would be expected to be able to critically evaluate the quality of teaching and learning. Do we have that same expectation around senior leaders being able to critically evaluate the quality of effective SEND provision?

A better comparator than a curriculum area would be safeguarding. Much like the SENCO is the lead on SEND, there is a designated safeguarding lead (DSL). However, school leaders would not claim they do not need to have any expertise in safeguarding because they employ a DSL. It is a well-established principle that safeguarding is everybody's responsibility, with a particular expectation on leaders to ensure this is understood and that effective practice is embedded. If schools are serious about inclusion, then a similar commitment and approach should be in place for SEND.

So, should the SENCO be a SEND expert? Well . . . both the SENCO and the Headteacher should have some SEND expertise, and this should be developing over time. To deliver a whole school approach to inclusion, SEND must be everyone's responsibility.

## Reflection Questions

1. What are the ways in which a SENCO can improve their expertise over time?
2. Is it reasonable to expect all Headteachers to have a minimum level of knowledge about SEND? If so, what should this include?

## The Depth, Breadth and Reach of the SENCO Role

This chapter has so far emphasised the variability of the SENCO role between settings, and this has been presented as an issue. However, it is helpful to reflect on whether we would actually want all SENCO roles to be exactly the same. There are good arguments that personalised and contextualised provision can empower all learners, particularly those with SEND, if the right resources are available (Lindner and Schwab, 2020; Tsai et al., 2020), so surely we ought to welcome variation in the SENCO role to realise this, albeit with some minimum set of expectations. Much like we should be thinking about pupils with SEND as individuals rather than as one homogenous group (Boddison, 2021, p. 16), the same is true of SENCOs.

The complexity, evolution and variability of the SENCO role raise important questions related to the professional identity of SENCOs and their place within a wider community of SEND professionals. Variability within the SENCO role and between different SENCOs can bring flexibility (Boddison, 2018, p. 23), but it can also bring isolation to a role which is already solitary in nature (Curran, 2019b). This is at odds with the expectations of Morewood (2018a), who argues that 'the SENCO should not be an isolated figure, but a key in-house consultant for all'. Sadly, it is too often the case that when the SENCO is called upon by colleagues in this way, it is a one-way transaction, with professional support from colleagues to the SENCO being less than forthcoming (Fitzgerald and Radford, 2022).

Fortunately, there are communities at a local and national level for SENCOs, and this can help to break down feelings of isolation. The professional body for SENCOs, nasen, has a SENCO Forum and multiple other online communities for specialist groups. Similarly, there are online communities within social media networks, such as Facebook and LinkedIn. Within school Trusts and local authorities, there are often SENCO networks and conferences to support knowledge exchange and professional development. A group of SENCOs in one such local network described it as 'therapeutic' and 'an opportunity to talk with people who really understand'. These networks are essential for SENCOs' wellbeing. In the words of one SENCO, 'It's the best job in the world, but one of the hardest, loneliest, most misunderstood roles in a school' (Curran and Boddison, 2021).

This discussion supports the wider literature in demonstrating the uniqueness and multi-faceted nature of the SENCO role in comparison to other school-based roles (Brewin and Knowler, 2023, p. 12; Curran and Boddison, 2021; Smith and Broomhead, 2019, Richards and Legarska, 2023, p. 134). This complexity extends beyond the SENCO role itself and impacts on related processes and people.

For example, accountability for SENCOs often lacks clarity and simplicity. Are SENCOs accountable to their line manager, to the Headteacher or to the SEND Governor? Perhaps SENCOs are truly accountable to parents/carers or to pupils with SEND? The likelihood is that the SENCO will be accountable to most, if not all, of these stakeholders as well as to others not listed. This creates an issue, since these different stakeholder groups have different needs and expectations, and balancing these is akin to serving multiple masters (Soan and Monsen, 2023, p. 107).

An illustration of the depth and breadth of knowledge that SENCOs need to have is the increasing expectation that they need to liaise with other vulnerable groups of pupils in a school (Curran, 2019c, p. 14). For example, the SENCO will need to coordinate with the staff member leading on pupil premium to ensure that resources and interventions are aligned for learners from disadvantaged backgrounds who also have SEND (Boddison, 2021, p. 40). Similarly, the SENCO will need to liaise with the designated teacher for looked-after children (LAC) and the designated safeguarding lead (DSL) to ensure that any SEND provision put in place is appropriate in the context of pupils' wider circumstances (Tutt, 2016a, p. 42; Curran et al., 2018). Even when it comes to pupils with English as an additional language (EAL), the SENCO is likely to be directly involved, not least because speech, language and communication needs (SLCN) are often conflated or confused with EAL (Bosse et al., 2019, p. 22).

> The role of the SENCO spans both the micro and the macro; covering people, provisions and budgets, SENCOs have the fullest involvement with individual students, run the largest department, and take responsibility for whole school leadership issues such as lesson design by teachers.
>
> (Sobel, 2018, p. 84)

Whilst each element of this quote is not universally true in every school, it is hard to argue with the underpinning principle. The depth and breadth of the SENCO role is enormous and should not be underestimated. The SENCO role has tentacles that reach into every part of a school and its day-to-day provision. It is hard to think of any other role in a school that has such an extensive reach.

Given the breadth, depth and reach of the SENCO role, it is hardly surprising that workload is seen by many as excessive (Smith, 2022a, p. 11; Tirraoro, 2018; Rozsahegyi and Lambert, 2023, p. 43), with paperwork and administration at the heart of the issue (Curran et al., 2018). The SEND Code of Practice (DfE and DoH, 2015) states that there should be 'sufficient time and resources' for SENCOs to undertake the role, but it stops short of providing any guidance on how much time is needed. This is likely a consequence of the variability of the SENCO role as discussed earlier in this chapter. Despite this, Curran (2019c, pp. 118–123) does set out some guidance on the amount of protected time that SENCOs should be allocated. The guidance draws on multiple parameters including school phase, school size and the proportion of pupils with SEND to determine to appropriate amount of time. This ranges from 1.5 days per week to more than five days per week, the latter clearly requiring a second qualified SENCO or an assistant SENCO with whom to share the load.

Another demanding and time-consuming aspect of the SENCO role is building external relationships. For example, the SENCO is expected to maintain effective relationships with a broad range of external agencies as well as understanding their various policies, processes, procedures and expectations. In addition to the relationships with statutory services, SENCOs are also expected to be familiar with the work of many third sector organisations and to engage with those offering relevant services (Middleton and Kay, 2020, p. 113; Tutt, 2011).

Returning to the expectations of SENCOs as set out in the most recent SEND Code of Practice (DfE and DoH, 2015, pp. 108–109), there is significant support for the notion that this is an absolute minimum expectation rather than a final destination (Richards and Legarska, 2023, p. 138; Hallet and Hallet, 2017; Clarke and Done, 2021). Going beyond statutory expectations requires both time and resource, neither of which SENCOs have enough of (Curran et al., 2018).

---

### Box 1.5  SEND magnets

One of the factors that can negatively impact on the SENCO role is the relative lack of strategic desire to be a school with a good reputation for meeting the needs of learners with SEND. O'Brien (2016, p. 8) makes the point that schools are rightly loud and proud when it comes to improving the life chances of children from disadvantaged backgrounds, but when it comes to SEND, there appears to be more reluctance. Schools fear getting reputation for meeting the needs of children with SEND, lest they become a 'SEND magnet' (Boddison, 2018, p. 23).

A school becomes a 'SEND magnet' when families in the local area know that this is the school that your children should attend if you want their needs to be fully met. The unintended consequence is that the 'SEND magnet' school then becomes overwhelmed with demand for its provision, and so it struggles to meet the needs of pupils with SEND.

At the same time, the neighbouring school to the 'SEND magnet' ends up having disproportionately fewer children with SEND. Even if parents/carers want to send their children to the neighbouring school, a conversation might well occur during an open evening, where a staff member comments that 'there is a school up the road which is far better equipped to meet your child's needs'. Once such comments are made, even if done so with the best of intentions, the young person with SEND and their family could easily interpret this as an indication that the school does not want them. It is effectively exclusion prior to the point of admission.

This scenario highlights why the SEN notional budget is a flawed approach to providing core SEND funding to schools. The risk is that schools are financially penalised for being inclusive and that, conversely, they are financially better off by limiting the number of pupils with SEND who are enrolled.

Those schools that do actively welcome pupils with SEND can sometimes end up in a situation where their inclusivity inadvertently creates a further imbalance between themselves and other less inclusive schools. For example, if a school has pupils with physical disabilities, it may need to adapt its infrastructure to ensure it is fully accessible. Consequently, it can become the only school in an area which is accessible to pupils with similar disabilities. This is a self-fulfilling prophecy which further magnetises the SEND magnets.

The other consequence of creating a 'SEND magnet' is that families who are primarily focused on academic outcomes may not send their children to the inclusive school. Their perception could be that an inclusive school is not sufficiently focused on academic excellence. The irony is that the knock-on decision of parents/carers to not send their academically able children to the 'SEND magnet' school is likely to negatively impact on academic outcomes, for which school leaders are accountable. It also skews the needs profile of the pupil population, resulting in Ofsted asking questions about why the neighbouring school has far higher rates of progress and attainment, given that pupils are drawn from the same local demographic.

The implications for policy makers are clear. Schools should be incentivised to be inclusive, not penalised. This is not solely about financial incentives and penalties but also about the system of accountability for schools. Ofsted should recognise and reward inclusive practice. Ultimately, no school should be graded outstanding by Ofsted, unless they can demonstrate unequivocally that they are inclusive (Boddison, 2019a).

## Reflection Questions

1. How can schools be incentivised to be inclusive? If an incentive is needed, should we still think of them as inclusive schools?
2. Should Ofsted have a more nuanced approach to inspecting schools with a significantly greater-than-average volume and complexity of needs?

## *Going Beyond the Statutory Requirements*

For SENCOs to have any chance of being successful in the role, there should be a clarity of expectations from the outset (Middleton and Kay, 2021), and SENCOs should be given sufficient agency in the role. As it stands, the expectations of SENCOs as set out in the SEND Code of Practice (DfE and DoH, 2015, pp. 108–109) are too vague (Robinson et al., 2018). The expectations of SENCOs are also insufficient, not least because one of the key stakeholder groups, parents/carers, are not confident that the current system works (Boddison and Soan, 2021). Given the complexities of the SENCO role, any list of expectations is likely to fall short. However, Purdy and Boddison (2018, p. 331) include the following advice for teachers, which might be a useful and complementary starting point for SENCOs looking to further improve quality-first teaching:

- Consider the need to make adaptations to the learning environment, the task set and your teaching style, rather than focusing solely on the child's learning characteristics.
- Be aware of the particular targets set in a child's support plan and plan your teaching to facilitate the meeting of those targets. This necessitates knowledge and understanding of the particular child, their needs and the barriers to their learning. . . . You should also remember to take into account the whole-school provision, which might include, for instance, evidence-based group interventions for literacy, numeracy or social skills support.
- Remember that you are not alone: ask for advice and support from more experienced teachers, and especially from the school SENCO.
- Always seek the support of the child's parents/carers as 'equal partners', as they can offer unrivalled insights into the child's needs and also help to reinforce at home the strategies you are implementing in class.
- Take every opportunity to develop your own skills and understanding through professional development courses and/or membership of professional organisations (e.g., nasen).
- Remember that each child with SEN is unique. Although knowledge of key policy and legislation is a requirement, and although an understanding of key aspects of common SEN is very useful, it is crucial that you get to know the individual strengths and needs of each individual child . . . including an understanding of their lives outside school.

## *The SEND Governor*

Boddison (2021) provides a thorough insight into the role of the SEND Governor, which will not be replicated here. Nevertheless, it is useful to reflect briefly on the main duties of the SEND Governor and the aspects of the role where it interacts with the SENCO. Much like the SENCO role, the expectations of the SEND Governor role have been strengthened with each iteration of statutory guidance.

The 2001 SEN Code of Practice first introduced the notion of a SEN Governor, but the guidance did not mandate schools to have the role and suggested it could be the responsibility of a sub-committee rather than a named individual (DfES, 2001, p. 5). The Code also stipulated that governing bodies had 'important statutory duties towards pupils with special educational needs' (DfES, 2001, p. 10). However, the tendency was for all governance of SEND to be done via the routine support and challenge of the Headteacher, rather than with the SENCO directly, unless they already happened to be a regular attendee at governor meetings. In addition to the SEN Governor, the Code also placed a duty on governing bodies to appoint a 'responsible person' whose role was to inform teachers if one of their pupils had a statement of special educational needs (DfES, 2001, p. 5). Although this is clearly an operational responsibility and likely to fall within the remit of the modern SENCO, the Code was somewhat confusing in that it suggested the Chair of Governors might be the 'responsible person'.

It was the SENCO Regulations (HM Government, 2008) where the expectation of the SENCO and the SEND Governor working together directly became more explicit. The regulations set out that the governing body should determine the key responsibilities of the SENCO and monitor their effectiveness. As Browning (2016) puts it, the SENCO and the SEND Governor should work together as a 'dynamic duo'. Interestingly, the most recent SEND Code of Practice (DfE and DoH, 2015) does not explicitly reference the SEND Governor role. In fact, the word 'governor' is only mentioned four times across all 292 pages. However, it is governing bodies that have the overall accountability for ensuring that their schools are inclusive and have effective provision in place for all pupils, including pupils with SEND.

---

## Box 1.6 The SEND Governor role description

In the absence of a clear role description for the SEND Governor within the statutory guidance, one has been provided here. This may be useful when the board is appointing a SEND Governor or as a reference for the SEND Governor once in post.

**Role Title:**      SEND Governor
**Responsible To:**    Chair of Governors
**Role Purpose:**     To monitor the school's arrangements for SEND. To provide a voice for the SENCO at board level and to ensure that the needs of learners with SEND are considered as part of strategic decision-making. To support and challenge all senior leaders (including the SENCO) to verify that the needs of learners with SEND are being met effectively.

### Duties and Responsibilities:

In addition to the standard duties of effective governance, the SEND governor role includes:

- Regular meetings with the SENCO (termly or half-termly)
- Ensuring the annual SEND report (written by school leaders) receives appropriate consideration at board level and that suitable strategic decisions are made as a consequence
- Supporting the Chair of Governors to make certain that the SEND responsibilities of the board are fully discharged
- Reminding the wider board to consider the impact of their decisions on learners with SEND, particularly where this may not be immediately obvious or explicit ('Think SEND!')
- Raising SEND and inclusion issues at board level, typically in consultation with the Headteacher and the SENCO
- Monitoring the culture, values and ethos of the school *to ensure they remain inclusive*
- Checking that the school makes good use of financial resources (as well as the SEN notional budget) including:
  - assessing the impact of SEND spend
  - ensuring that SEND is appropriately considering in budget setting and other budget discussions
  - establishing that value for money is being achieved

- Holding the Headteacher to account in relation to:
  - ° the experiences of learners with SEND
  - ° outcomes for learners with SEND
  - ° the effective deployment of the SENCO and other SEND staff
- Checking the school has a designated SENCO and, if appropriate, that they have (or are working towards) the National Award for SEN Coordination as well as access to any additional training they may need.
- Involvement in the appointment of a new SENCO or Assistant SENCO (or Trustee involvement in the appointment of a new Director of Inclusion in a Trust)
- Monitoring the SEND training received by staff and board members to ensure it is sufficient, responsive and impactful
- Checking that the board understands the school's profile of needs and that this is used to inform strategic decision-making (for example there should be a strong positive correlation between training, financial expenditure and the school's profile of needs)
- Ensuring the board is familiar with chapter six in the SEND Code of Practice (DfE and DoH, 2015, pp. 91–110)
- Checking that the quality of SEND provision is good, that learners with SEND feel included and that coproduction is effective (for example through the coordination of SEND learning walks)
- Prompting the board to routinely check the school is compliant with key legislation, such as the Equality Act 2010 and the Children and Families Act 2014
- Ensuring the school has a high-quality SEN Information Report, Accessibility Plan and SEND Policy as well as ensuring that all school policies are 'SEND-supportive' and meet statutory requirements
- Requesting that data sets (for example attendance and progress data) presented to the board are routinely broken down to include learners with SEND, including by type of need where appropriate

In order to perform this role well, the SEND governor is expected to:

- Attend regular training on SEND and inclusion
- Take proactive steps to remain up-to-date on the local, regional and national policy context for SEND and any associated processes and procedures
- Develop a good understanding of the school's approach to SEND provision and inclusive practice
- Be involved with the school's self-evaluation of SEND provision
- Have a thorough understanding of the views of all key stakeholders in relation to SEND (for example children, families, staff, volunteers, governors and the local authority).

## Person Specification:

The SEND governor should have:

- A current role on the board as a governor (although an expert external candidate can be appointed to undertake the role as an associate governor)
- A commitment to inclusion, equality and diversity
- A commitment to learn and improve
- An interest in SEND and inclusion
- The necessary time and availability to undertake the role effectively
- Knowledge of key SEND and inclusion legislation (or a willingness to develop it)
- Professional qualifications or personal experience in SEND or inclusive education (desirable)

## Reflection Questions

1. What is your assessment of this role description for the SEND Governor? What is missing? What would you change or remove?
2. How could the effectiveness of the relationships between the SENCO, the SEND Governor and the Headteacher be assessed?

Over the past decade, it is fair to say that the expectations of SEND provision in schools have not been sufficiently embedded within wider changes to education policy. For example, the SEND reforms (Gov UK, 2014) failed to have sufficient relevance to the academisation of the school system in England. If the pathway to academisation had explicitly included a requirement to have outstanding SEND provision, then the current educational landscape and priorities might look very different.

## Other Developments Related to the SENCO Role

This chapter has made multiple references to the National Award for SEN Coordination, but the most recent SEND green paper sets out the government's intention to introduce a new SENCO National Professional Qualification (NPQ) to replace the existing requirements (HM Government, 2022, p. 14; Soan and Monsen, 2023, p. 83). Some believe that it is difficult to appoint SENCOs under the current system (Sobel, 2018, p. 50), and this might be due to the Masters-level expectation of the National Award for SEN Coordination. Moving to the NPQ does have the advantage of positioning the SENCO role more centrally as part of the wider suite of NPQs as a senior leadership role in schools. However, transitioning the qualification from postgraduate level to undergraduate level is arguably de-professionalising the role (Soan and Monsen, 2023, p. 93).

The proposed change has echoes of the transition from university-led to school-led teacher education, which remains problematic and is arguably exacerbating the teacher shortage issues in England (Fazackerley, 2022; Walker, 2023). It will be important to learn the lessons of the past to ensure there are sufficient qualified SENCOs available. The other challenge of having reduced academic input is the risk of the NPQ becoming a closed system void of external reflection. It will be important for SENCOs to retain the opportunity to stay abreast of the latest thinking and debate in SEND. One potential gap in the government's proposed changes is whether there should be a mandated qualification aimed at Trust-level SENCOs, who are providing leadership to multiple SENCOs across multiple schools.

At a policy level, there are advocates of schools having a protected, full-time role for SENCOs (Lamb, 2021). If we assume that employing a SENCO on the leadership team costs an average of £60k (inclusive of on-costs), then providing a funded, full-time SENCO in each of the 21,262 maintained schools in England (DfE, 2023d) would cost the taxpayer around £1.3bn per year.

There is an argument that if government provided new money to fully fund a full-time SENCO for every school in the country, this would (i) allow the existing financial resource in schools that is being spent on the SENCO to be redistributed and (ii) increase the level of ordinarily available provision nationally, thereby reducing the demand and cost of specialist provision. On this latter point, it should be made clear that the impact would be felt most acutely by pupils on the cusp of mainstream and specialist provision. There would still be a requirement for specialist provision for those with the most complex needs.

If every school had a full-time SENCO, this would provide a good opportunity to reinforce their leadership status as standard and would allow for a more consistent understanding of the SENCO role. The Department for Education could use the school census to collate a central list of every SENCO in England, and then this could be used to communicate policy updates and changes to statutory guidance. It could also be used to disseminate government-funded SEND resources, thereby helping to ensure that public money is spent well through maximising the availability and impact of the resources. One could imagine national online SEND conferences attended by every SENCO in the country. SENCOs would no longer feel isolated, but instead part of a vibrant peer community.

Critics would likely argue that providing a full-time SENCO for every school in the country would be inequitable and a waste of public money. Schools have different scales, complexities and contexts. The smallest schools may not need nor want a full-time SENCO, and the largest schools may need more than one person in the SENCO role. The challenge for government is that any attempt to differentiate the approach at a national level introduces complexity and cost, thereby reducing the amount of money that goes directly towards developing SEND provision in schools. The best value for money is likely to come from policies at the national level that are simple to understand and to implement.

## Conclusion

The intention of this chapter was to explore the SENCO role and to peek behind the curtain into the secret lives of SENCOs. The SENCO role has developed over time into a more strategic role, but it remains complex and varied. When it comes to the effectiveness of SENCOs, it is clear that Headteachers and Governors have an important role to play in helping the SENCO to drive a whole-school approach to SEND and inclusion.

## Reflection Questions

1. Irrespective of whether the SENCO is part of the senior leadership team, how can the SENCO ensure that they have sufficient strategic influence to drive a whole-school approach to SEND and inclusion?
2. Given the evolution of the SENCO role over the past 20 years, how do you think the SENCO role will change over the next 20 years?

## Suggested Resources

1. The *SENCO Induction Handbook* is a government-funded resource designed for SENCOs who are new to the role and have not yet undertaken any development or received any SENCO qualifications. It was commissioned by Whole School SEND and provides an excellent foundation to the SENCO role as well as being a helpful reference guide for experienced SENCOs. Headteachers and SEND Governors have also found the handbook useful as it has helped them to better understand the day-to-day requirements of the SENCO role.
   www.wholeschoolsend.org.uk/resources/senco-induction-pack-revised-edition
2. The *Teacher Handbook: SEND* is a government-funded resource designed to support teachers to embed inclusive practice in the classrooms. It is a reference book that provides phase-specific, subject-specific and condition-specific guidance on scaffolding and quality-first teaching. This is a useful resource for SENCOs providing support and development to individual classroom teachers.
   www.wholeschoolsend.org.uk/resources/teacher-handbook-send

# 2  The Alternatives to School Exclusions

The disproportionate rate of exclusions of pupils with SEND is a national issue. In this chapter, England's data on exclusions over time will be explored, and consideration will be given to the alternatives to exclusion. In particular, there will be a deep dive into a school that has a zero-exclusions policy, exploring what that actually means in practice and whether it is a realistic approach for more schools to adopt.

## Exclusions: The National Picture

Let us begin by considering what can be gleaned from the publicly available national data sets on exclusions published by the Department for Education (DfE, 2023b). It is typical for analysis of these data sets to focus immediately on the number of exclusions and how this varies over time. An alternative approach is to report on the number of schools who have not permanently excluded or suspended any pupils and to see whether this number is increasing or decreasing over time. This data is provided each academic term (autumn, spring and summer), and Figure 2.1 shows the trend from late 2016 to the end of 2022 (the most recently available published data at the time of writing).

The positive news is that there are regularly more than 10,000 schools with zero permanent exclusions and zero suspensions (zero-exclusion schools). However, these are not necessarily the same 10,000+ schools each term. During the global pandemic, when many pupils were accessing education online rather than physically attending school, the number of zero-exclusion schools spiked at more than 20,000, but this quickly returned to pre-pandemic levels by summer 2021. Perhaps the most worrying news is that there is a slow but steady linear downward trend in the number of zero-exclusion schools. This reduction is occurring at an average rate of approximately 250 schools per year. If this trend continues, the data suggests there will be no zero-exclusion schools left in just over 40 years.

Extending the analysis further, Figure 2.2 considers the prevalence of pupils with SEND as a proportion of those pupils who have been permanently excluded. From 2006 to 2012, the data shows a challenging picture where more than seven in ten permanent exclusions were for pupils with SEND. From 2012 to 2018, this proportion dropped, and for the past few years it has remained steady at around 45% of permanent exclusions being for pupils with SEND. This is concerning and disproportionate given that around one in six pupils has SEND (based on the most recently available census data from January 2023).

Further exploration of the national data also suggests there is a growing problem with rising numbers of suspensions of children aged 5 or younger (DfE, 2023b). Figure 2.3 is a summary of national data from the Department for Education, which shows a steady rise in the number of young children being suspended since 2008. There was a brief period of fewer suspensions during the global pandemic, but even then more than 5000 5-year olds per year were being suspended each year. The most recent data available has the highest number of suspensions for young children in recent history, building on the pre-pandemic rising trend.

Given that behaviour is a communication of need, it is important to consider whether these young children are being suspended as a result of unmet, and potentially unidentified, special educational needs. It should also be acknowledged that it can be challenging to identify SEND in young children since it is sometimes hard to distinguish between typical variations in early childhood development and delayed development that is a consequence of unmet needs.

In some schools and settings, the COVID pandemic is cited as one of the reasons why exclusions are rising. For example, there are some school-based staff who share the notion that missed education and a lack of routines have resulted in poor behaviour, which in some cases has led to exclusion. Whist this may be a factor in the increased number of exclusions, the truth

DOI: 10.4324/9781032634807-2

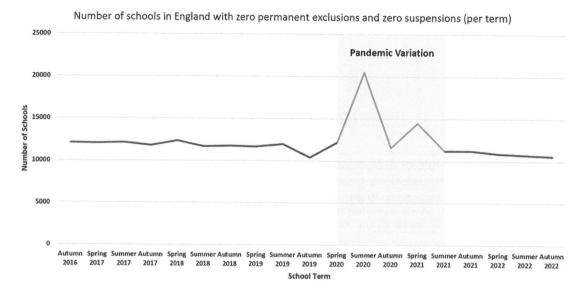

*Figure 2.1* The number of schools in England with zero permanent exclusions and zero suspensions (per term)

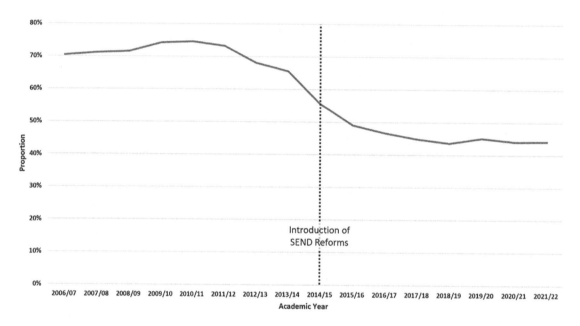

*Figure 2.2* The proportion of permanent exclusions over time who are pupils with SEND

is that the rising trend of exclusions was occurring well before the global pandemic as was the disproportionate number of pupils with SEND being excluded. The longer-term issues are more likely a result of years of resource limitations as well as reductions to systemic support such as 'early help' and SLCN (speech, language and communication needs) services.

The point made around children's needs changing as a consequence of the pandemic is worthy of further consideration. For example, children who were babies or toddlers during the pandemic are more likely to experience SLCN. Not only did they have limited, if any, access to communication with other children but for the communication they did observe, people would likely have been wearing masks. Added to this, significant numbers of children did not have the standard two-year check undertaken by health visitors, which has traditionally been an opportunity to support the early identification of SEND. More generally, as this cohort of COVID babies moves through the school system, there may be long-term disparities between those who attended nursery during the pandemic and those who did not.

In summary, the national picture is not positive. Both suspensions and permanent exclusions are rising over time with a disproportionate number of children and young people with SEND being excluded. Exclusions of young children are also increasing, with no evidence that systemic changes to the education system will reverse this rising trend.

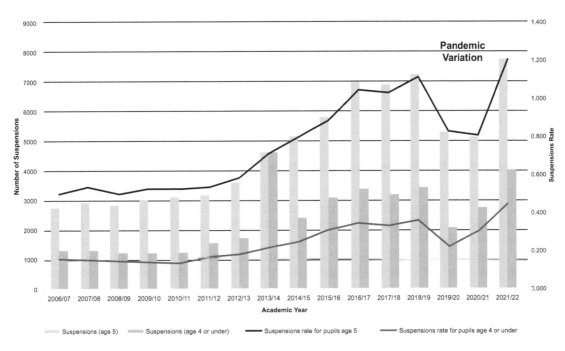

*Figure 2.3* Suspensions of young children over time

## No Option but to Exclude?

A reasonable assumption is that those working in schools and settings do so because they care about children and young people, and they want them to have a high-quality education. The teaching profession is often described as a 'calling', with plenty of critics arguing that the pay is insufficient. This is important because it tells us that teachers and school leaders do not come into the role with the intention of excluding pupils from school. Furthermore, anecdotal evidence suggests it is common for school leaders to say that excluding a child is something they do reluctantly and only when they feel they have 'no other option'. From the SENCO perspective, they can sometimes find themselves trying to convince the Headteacher not to exclude a child, whilst the Headteacher feels their hands are tied. Box 2.1 considers this scenario and explores the various affordances and constraints that could impact on the Headteacher's ultimate decision about whether or not to exclude.

---

**Box 2.1 Charlie's situation**

Persistent disruptive behaviour is one of the reasons given when a child is suspended or permanently excluded from school. Consider a situation where a 13-year-old boy called Charlie regularly leaves the classroom and runs around school. Sometimes, this results in damage to school property or other children being hurt. On one occasion, Charlie injures a member of staff who was trying to stop him running around the school site.

A small number of teaching staff have threatened to resign if they have to teach Charlie as they say they feel unsafe. Another teacher has been in the Headteacher's office crying and upset about the stress she feels when Charlie is in her class. The teacher who was injured is insisting that Charlie is excluded and has consulted his union for advice. In addition to this, a formal complaint has been received from the parents of a child who Charlie hurt whilst running around the school on a previous occasion, and they are demanding 'justice'.

The Headteacher feels they have no option but to exclude Charlie. However, the Headteacher is aware that Charlie is on the SEND register and decides to consult the SENCO before making any final decisions.

**SENCO/Reflection Questions**

The SENCO is asked two questions:

1. How should the staff respond when Charlie is running around the school site?
2. How can the school's approach develop over time to reduce the likelihood of this type of situation reoccurring?

## Responding to the Immediate Situation

In considering how to respond to the immediate situation outlined in Box 2.1, there is plenty of other information not included in the scenario that would be useful to know. For example, we know that Charlie has SEND, but no detail is given about what type of needs Charlie has and whether or not he has an EHC (Education, Health and Care) plan. Similarly, we do not know the wider context of the school or Charlie's circumstances. Therefore, any suggested response should be seen as a starting point to be adapted depending on the individual circumstances.

It may sound obvious, but there is no one approach that will work in every situation. If there was, everybody would be doing it already. A level of pragmatism is needed, and school leaders should not be afraid to challenge the status quo where it makes sense to do so. To be clear, policies still need to be followed as they are in place for a reason, but school leaders often have scope in how they choose to implement policies in practice.

So what should the immediate response be for this type of scenario? Interviews with SENCOs and leaders in specialist settings suggest there are five important steps to be included as part of any response, as shown in Figure 2.4.

1.  *Change the narrative*
    The way in which we describe a situation can materially affect how staff respond to it. If we take Charlie's scenario as an example, then one school leader might describe this as 'Charlie has absconded from the classroom' whilst another might describe it as 'Charlie is trying to find a safe space'.

    Changing the narrative in this way is much easier when the most senior member of staff in the situation are themselves regulated. It is therefore helpful for school leaders to have a level of self-awareness about their own emotional state.

    A revised narrative can directly impact on what the priority is for the member of staff leading on the response to the situation. For example, is the immediate priority to regulate the

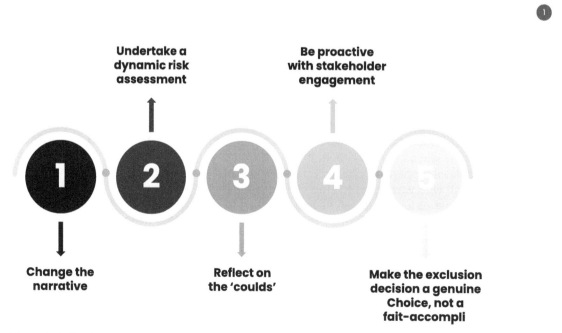

*Figure 2.4* Five important steps to be included as part of the immediate response to a dysregulated pupil displaying behaviours that may lead to an exclusion

situation or to manage the behaviour? In Charlie's case, is the priority to stop him running around the school, or is it about being seen to be tough on undesirable behaviour?

SENCOs have shared that in some instances, even when effective tactics for helping to regulate a child are known, there can be an active decision not to use those tactics for fear it might be seen as 'rewarding poor behaviour'. For example, it may be that a useful distraction technique for Charlie is playing with football stickers, but this might be discounted if it is seen as something Charlie enjoys rather than a consequence for his behaviour. The immediate priority should be focused on supporting Charlie to regulate his emotional state and to keep him and others safe.

2. *Undertake a dynamic risk assessment*

In a dysregulated situation the pre-determined risks and mitigations may no longer be relevant. It can be helpful to rapidly undertake a dynamic risk assessment to help inform how the situation is approached.

In the moment some things to consider are the following:

- What is the level of risk? If high, respond immediately. If low, can we move away, redirect or resolve?
- What are they likely to do next?
- Who is around?
- Where are the exits, or is there anything in the way of the exit?
- Are there any items that could cause serious harm?
- Is it a key time of day?
- Who is the person who knows them well?
- Is there a safe space nearby?
- What strategy is likely to work? (e.g., proximity, talking, connection)
- What strategy will likely make it worse?
- Who is in my support network, and how can I get the right support?

In Charlie's situation, a dynamic risk assessment would consider the new risks arising as a result of him running around the school as well as any emerging risks from the different possible staff responses. For example, if Charlie is running around the school corridors and kicking doors, would running after him or trying to intercept him increase or decrease the risk to him and to others? In some schools, the corridors form a circle in any case, so running after Charlie makes little sense and is more likely to escalate rather than de-escalate the situation. On the other hand, if Charlie is heading for the school kitchens or the science labs, the risks may require a more direct intervention in order to keep him safe.

3. *Reflect on the 'coulds'*

SENCOs describe a sort of autopilot that can occur when responding to dysregulated situations. They shared accounts of teachers and other school-based staff instinctively doing what they think they *should* do rather than reflecting on the things they *could* do. The advice from SENCOs is to stop for a moment to reflect on what options they actually have.

For example, the staff member might consider whether or not they are the best person to deal with the incident. Children will respond better or worse to certain people, and this should be a key factor in determining who is best placed to lead in helping them to regulate their emotions. SENCOs often have excellent insights into such relationships for pupils with SEND, and their input at this stage could be invaluable.

Returning to Charlie's situation, it may be that he gets on better with female staff rather than male staff, or younger staff rather than older staff. Equally, it may be that Charlie's relationship with specific staff members rules them in or out. For instance, if there is a curriculum area that Charlie struggles with, then there is a chance that his adverse emotional connection with that subject might affect how he perceives the subject teacher. Similarly, if there is a senior member of staff who regularly picks Charlie up whilst on-call, this could work either way. It might be a helpful relationship because Charlie sees this member of staff as somebody who listens to them.

Conversely, it might be a difficult relationship because Charlie associates this person as being a figure of authority who appears only when they are in trouble.

Extending this further, the most senior person involved in an incident is not always the most appropriate to respond to it, but that does not mean they need to disengage completely. It is likely that the most senior person is the one with the necessary influence to steer the situation to a positive outcome. Therefore, senior staff responding to such situations should carefully consider how they deploy themselves and their colleagues. This is not dissimilar to teachers considering how they deploy themselves and their teaching assistants in the classroom, albeit that is for learning needs rather than emotional or behavioural needs.

Is this the right place to address the issue? Children are often hyper-aware of their environments and how they are perceived by their peers. That being said, is there a better place or space to use to de-escalate a child or situation, and how are you able to do this? A more effective strategy may be to work with a child prior to an incident and discuss a safe space that they may use. Speaking to them in a dysregulated state is unlikely to be successful, but giving them a safe space to regulate can more easily provide opportunity to de-escalate and often resolves the situation more effectively.

Could you also not respond at all to the situation (if safe to do so)? On some occasions, behaviour is attention seeking, and if that undesirable behaviour gets the attention the child needs, then we have inadvertently reinforced the unwanted behaviour. A more effective strategy may be to give a preferred task to the child which stops the behaviour escalating as they become engaged in this more appropriate task. There are risks with this approach as it is possible that children may escalate to worse behaviour if they do not feel they are receiving the response they need.

4. *Be proactive with stakeholder engagement*

Much of the discussion about responding to the immediate situation has centred on the role of the SENCO and of school leaders more broadly. However, there are other stakeholders who need to be considered, not least the parents and the teachers who are pushing for Charlie to be excluded as well as any pupils at the school impacted by Charlie's behaviour.

Before considering these three groups specifically for Charlie's situation, there is a more generic framework that can be used for quickly categorising stakeholders. This framework is known as a 'power and interest matrix', and it provides a useful starting point for how particular groups might be approached, as shown in Figure 2.5.

When it comes to engaging the three stakeholder groups of parents, families and pupils, the school's culture, ethos and values are likely to influence how easy or difficult this task may be. For example, if the school has values that prioritise academic excellence at any cost, this will limit the scope of the Headteacher to avoid an exclusion. An ethos that balances educational ambition with individual needs will be helpful in managing the expectations of different school community stakeholder groups.

The advice from SENCOs is not to consider all parents as one homogenous group as their power and interest will differ from person to person. Despite this caution from SENCOs, they do also suggest that there will be some things that are likely to be common across many different sets of parents. For example, it should not be a surprise when parents are frustrated if their child has been harmed in some way by another pupil, particularly when there is little they can do about it. In this type of situation, it is suggested that school leaders give plenty of time for parents, but that they do not give at all on their inclusive school values. For example, a parent may be pushing for an exclusion, but the school's values and policies might suggest that is a last resort rather than a go-to response.

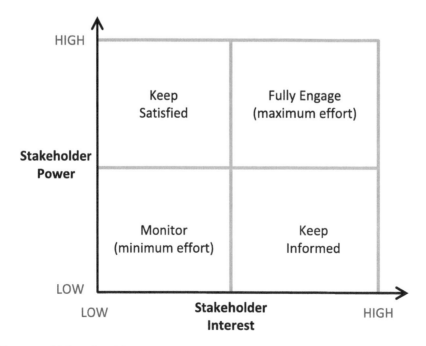

*Figure 2.5* Power and interest matrix

By not excluding children like Charlie, it is possible that Headteachers may fear complaints to governors, reputational damage to the school or an adverse impact on academic outcomes if other parents decide to transfer their children to another school. However, it is important that school leaders hold their nerve and do what is right for that individual pupil. One Headteacher articulated this as getting back to the 'first principles of education' and described how he asks parents in such situations what their dying wish would be for their child. He notes that they never say it would be to have 'good GCSE grades' and is more typically about their children being happy and living fulfilled lives. He argues that this can be a useful hook in helping parents to see beyond academic outcomes alone.

When it comes to school-based staff members, ensuring alignment to the school's inclusive values becomes important once again. When teachers have a dysregulated pupil in their class causing disruption regularly, they will understandably be concerned about the impact of this on other pupils and themselves. This might be the educational impact, but they will equally be mindful of keeping everybody safe. The following statements are common ways in which teachers on the receiving end of challenging behaviour might express their concerns to the Headteacher:

*"The child is unteachable"*

*"It would be impossible for them to return to my classroom"*

*"There has been a fundamental breakdown of trust"*

*"The relationship has completely broken down"*

*"They're not a mainstream child"*

*"You are putting the needs of children ahead of the needs of staff"*

*"We focus a lot of pupil wellbeing, but not enough on staff wellbeing"*

*"I don't get paid enough to get spat at"*

*"I don't come to work every day to be abused"*

For school leaders responding to this type of feedback from their staff, there is a balance to be struck between the needs of the dysregulated pupil, other pupils and the teacher. When such concerns are raised, the timing of any conversation between the Headteacher and the teacher should ideally be independent of the individual incident, so not part of the immediate response if at all possible. This will ensure both parties can make proactive strategic decisions rather than reactive, emotionally-driven decisions.

This conversation can be a good opportunity to consider reflective questions that relate to the teacher's own lived experiences and how these contribute to their current perspectives, expectations and responses. For example, the Power Threat Meaning Framework (Johnstone and Boyle, 2018) suggests the following:

- What has happened to you? (How has **Power** operated in your life?)
- How did it affect you? (What kind of **Threats** does this pose?)
- What sense did you make of it? (What is the **Meaning** of these situations and experiences to you?)
- What did you have to do to survive? (What kinds of **Threat Responses** are you using?)

This sort of thinking allows reflection, both from the person asking these questions and the one who is being supported. It is key not to focus too much on solving the situation at hand. For example, if a child has spat at a teacher, these questions provide the opportunity to look at how this behaviour has impacted the teacher linked to their previous life experiences.

This framework is primarily about the human need for justice and safe community. This can be especially hard for teachers to experience as they are often having to use power in the classroom, and with an individual seemingly seeking to undermine this power, it can unnerve even the most experienced professional.

After using the framework, the member of staff should be given the opportunity to realise that although there is a perceived threat, they as the leader in the classroom/school have all the power, and that the feeling of losing control is just that, a feeling. In these situations, it can be useful to have psychological supervision to support those individuals affected.

When the conversation between the Headteacher and classroom teacher does eventually happen, SENCOs suggest that the initial priority should be to agree what the issues are. Without consensus on what the problem is that needs to be solved, there is an increased risk that any agreed actions will be ineffective.

Discussing these types of conversations, one Headteacher talked about the need to ensure that accountability remains with the classroom teacher to ensure that all pupils in their class make progress. She was adamant that the answer was rarely to remove the child from the class as next year the teacher may have the same issue with another child, then another child and so forth. Instead, she advocates an approach where the SENCO and other school leaders build the capability and capacity of the teacher so they can better respond to the child's behaviour. In this conversation, she would ask the teacher, "What can I do that will make it possible for the child to be included in your classroom, both short-term and long-term?"

This Headteacher feels the answer often lies with teachers themselves, and she encourages them to reflect on the effectiveness of their approach to quality-first teaching. In particular, she works with teachers to develop a level of ordinarily available provision in the classroom that meets a broad range of needs by design rather than developing strategies for responding to specific behaviours. This includes ensuring that the deployment of support staff and other resources is working effectively.

When asked about Charlie's specific circumstances, this Headteacher suggested that, in addition to a dynamic risk assessment, the immediate response might include the establishment of a safe space for Charlie. She made the point that if the decision is made to exclude, it removes one set of anxieties and replaces them with another related to the return and subsequent reintegration of the pupil. She questions whether this adds any value beyond keeping up appearances that the school is tough on behaviour.

When discussing the behaviour with other children, it is important to get the balance right between explaining another child's difficulties and saying children should accept behaviour that makes them have an emotive response. It is useful to provide the children with information about what is happening and why, along with other strategies for them to use to deal with arising situations.

5.  *Make the exclusion a genuine choice, not a fait-accompli*

    Some Headteachers have what they describe as 'red lines for behaviour', which, when crossed, will automatically result in the child being excluded. One Headteacher said that any child assaulting another pupil or a member of staff would automatically be excluded and that he had no choice in the matter. Another Headteacher made a similar comment about vaping and smoking. The question is: Are these red lines solid or blurred? To what extent can Headteachers use their discretion without undermining their expectations around behaviour?

    A SENCO relayed a conversation they had with their Headteacher when a child had crossed one such red line, which in this case was bringing illegal drugs into the school. The Headteacher was adamant that this 10-year-old child must be suspended for three days. Given the wider circumstances, the SENCO was concerned that excluding them from the school community would only accelerate the child's involvement in other, more damaging communities such as those involving 'County Lines'. The Headteacher understood this but was concerned that not excluding them might set a dangerous precedent or inadvertently communicate to other pupils that such behaviour was acceptable.

    In this particular case, the SENCO was able to convince the Headteacher to change the narrative (as per step one), and the child was not suspended. They agreed that the behaviour was unacceptable, but they wanted to address the behaviour without damaging the child's relationship with the school in the long term. They took the view that once the drugs were confiscated and the necessary authorities were informed, it was then their role to get the child back into the classroom as soon as possible, thereby minimising the amount of education missed and keeping them within a safe community. The message they communicated to the wider pupil population through their weekly assembly was that they might not always like or agree with what the children do, but they will always be welcome in the school community.

    Returning to Charlie one final time, we need to consider whether anybody really benefits in the long term when excluding a child with SEND. One could argue there are some immediate benefits, but given the longer term damage of the exclusion to Charlie, and potentially to society more broadly, this seems a disproportionately high price to pay. Will excluding Charlie result in improved behaviour, or will it merely proliferate the existing cycle of unwanted behaviours? And when we really think about it, is an exclusion a fair consequence for Charlie's behavioural choices, or does it represent him being punished for trying to communicate his unmet needs?

## Headteacher Red Lines

This notion of Headteacher red lines that automatically result in exclusion when crossed warrants further consideration. Firstly, how are such red lines set in the first place? Different schools have different sets of red lines, which means that for two children with the same behaviours, one would be excluded and one would not be excluded. Given the impact exclusion has on life chances, is such an arbitrary approach appropriate or even desirable?

The CEO of one school Trust shared how they implemented a policy whereby all exclusions had to be agreed with the CEO in a bid to create greater equity and to minimise the volume of exclusions. Whilst the overall number of exclusions was reduced, this policy also resulted in multiple Headteachers leaving the Trust citing that they were not given sufficient autonomy to run their own schools.

When governors and school leaders consider their strategic approach and policies for managing behaviour, there is published guidance available from the Department for Education to support them with this. This includes the statutory guidance on school exclusions and the non-statutory guidance on behaviour management. The guidance is helpful in many ways, but some of the underlying themes are problematic.

For example, one of the underlying themes appears to be that the needs of the school override the needs of any individual pupil. This suggests that the onus is on individual pupils to conform to the school's behavioural expectations rather than for the school to adopt an approach to managing behaviour that works for its pupils. This is problematic for pupils with SEND because it can lead to behaviour policies containing expectations that are impossible for them to meet due to their needs. Setting pupils with SEND up to fail in this way is arguably discriminatory.

In fairness, there are plenty of schools which state in their policies that behaviour is seen as a form of communication and that this should be reflected as part of any implementation. There are also plenty of schools which state in their policies that they must be implemented in the context of the needs of individual pupils. This scope for personalising the approach to behaviour is helpful, but it does call into question the whole notion of red lines. How can there be both automatic exclusion and an individualised approach at the same time? Whichever way you look at it, the red lines turn into 'pink blurred lines' quite quickly.

Some behaviour management policies specifically set out that a more inclusive and understanding approach should be taken for pupils with SEND. On the face of it, this seems like a positive contribution, but it poses two questions. Firstly, what about those pupils, particularly younger children, whose needs may not yet have been identified? Would they not also benefit from access to a more inclusive and understanding approach to behaviour management? Secondly, why restrict an inclusive and understanding approach to a subset of pupils in the first place? A better alternative would be to make the approach to behaviour management inclusive and understanding by design for all pupils. This would reflect the fact that all pupils will have different needs at different times. It would also emphasise 'difference over deficit', which is useful in embedding a culture of inclusion.

The Department for Education's guidance on school exclusions outlines the Headteacher's power to exclude or suspend. The word 'power' is important here since this implies that excluding a pupil is something a Headteacher *can* do rather than something they are *obliged* to do, even if the criteria for a potential exclusion are reached. Similarly, the guidance discusses the need for any decision to exclude to be 'lawful, reasonable, fair and proportionate'. Again, this provides an opportunity for Headteachers to apply discretion rather than compelling them to exclude. Headteachers do have the power to decide whether or not to exclude.

Interestingly, the guidance points out that suspension can be used as a mechanism to show 'a clear signal of what is unacceptable behaviour'. However, the guidance is less explicit about what other mechanisms Headteachers have available to them to provide an equivalent signal of what constitutes unacceptable behaviour, but arguably in a more constructive way than suspension.

Following a relational approach using restorative conferencing (similarly to those used by the police) can allow children to see the cause and effect of their actions, to allow them to make decisions around their actions and to consider any long-term implications.

Whilst this chapter has largely argued against school exclusion, there are school leaders, SENCOs and teachers who would argue that sometimes permanent exclusion or suspension is the right decision. For example, one SENCO in a mainstream school described how the only way to get a particular pupil with an EHC plan into a special school where they could access appropriate provision was for them to be permanently excluded from their mainstream school. Whilst in some ways this is understandable, it feels very much like penalising the child for the ineffectiveness of the system, not least because of the trauma that is known to come from such exclusions (King, 2016).

Another SENCO in a mainstream school argued that there is sometimes a case for using suspension to give a pupil 'the shock they need' to help get their behaviour back on track. However, she also made the point that such situations are rare and should only be done in consultation with the family, making it a 'done with' rather than a 'done to' decision.

The Headteacher at a specialist setting for SEMH made the point that some children and young people will deliberately try to be excluded, and so it is important to understand the reasons for this. For example, a young carer with a poor attendance record due to supporting a family member might be under pressure to attend school more regularly. If they are excluded, then the pressure to attend school disappears immediately, allowing them to care for their family member. This Headteacher points out that a tell-tale sign is when there is no benefit to the child's challenging behaviour. So, if a child just smashes a window for no apparent reason, there may be an underlying motive where exclusion itself is the benefit because they are a young carer.

---

### Box 2.2  At what point might a victim become a perpetrator?

Consider a 6-year-old child with SEMH needs called Conor, who lives in a household where domestic violence is prevalent. Furthermore, this violence is part of multi-generational trauma stemming from both sides of the family. Although the local authority are aware of the issues, social services have thus far been unable to remove Conor.

In school, Conor starts to display violent and threatening behaviours towards other pupils. One day, Conor comes into school with a metal BBQ skewer from home and threatens a girl called Joanna in his class. He tells Joanna he will stab her in the throat unless she steals money from home and gives it to him. A teacher sees the incident and intervenes before Joanna gets hurt, confiscating the skewer from Conor.

As part of the follow-up to this incident, the SENCO refers Conor to CAMHS for support. However, they refuse to support Conor because his mum will not engage with the CAMHS team. Despite the SENCO's argument that Conor's mum could herself be a victim or a perpetrator of domestic violence, the demand for CAMHS is such that they say they do not have the capacity to help.

The Headteacher at the school has informed Joanna's parents about the incident and is considering whether or not Conor should be excluded. The Headteacher and the SENCO discuss the incident for some time and conclude that Conor's worst offence was scaring Joanna. He has not physically harmed anybody, and he is himself a likely victim of domestic violence.

The Headteacher and the SENCO rule out excluding Conor as they believe this could be a catalyst for him switching from being a victim to becoming a victim who perpetrates. They feel they would be denying Conor the safe space of school and essentially forcing him to spend time in an environment that is likely to be fraught with danger. They deem the social norms of home to be problematic and argue it is in Conor's interests to remain in school.

### Reflection Questions

1. What is your opinion on the decision not to exclude Conor? Has the Headteacher struck the right balance between Conor's needs and Joanna's needs?
2. Given that he was not excluded for his behaviour, what other consequences should there be for Conor?
3. How could the school support and protect Joanna following this incident?
4. Why did CAMHS refuse to help Conor? Is that the right decision given their limited resources?
5. What else should the school be doing to support and protect Conor?

---

### *Developing the School's Approach Over Time*

In addition to the immediate responses to children who are dysregulated, it is useful for school leaders and SENCOs to also build up their capability and capacity strategically. This is important because being overly reactive is likely to impact on staff workload, particularly for the SENCO and for pastoral leaders. It will also impact on the effective use of resources since they might end up being used to respond to crises rather than for planned interventions to meet the needs of pupils with SEND.

As part of their strategic planning to be inclusive and to recognise behaviour as a communication of need, some schools have provided targeted CPD (continuing professional development) to teachers. For example, teachers may receive training so that they are better able to recognise the triggers that result in challenging behaviour for particular children. This can be very helpful, particularly when combined with strategies for teachers to respond early to situations, preventing the challenging behaviour from occurring in the first place.

Whilst an increasing number of teachers are skilled at recognising triggers, far fewer teachers have a good understanding of antecedents. This is something that routinely comes before the behaviour, but is not necessarily a direct trigger for the behaviour. An antecedent might be a smell, an action, a trigger or even a time of day. Much like a poker game, one might think of an antecedent as a 'tell' or an early indicator that the pupil is on a pathway to dysregulation. In the words of one SENCO, 'teachers have become too obsessed with triggers and not sufficiently obsessed with antecedents'.

Antecedents are easier to recognise the more you track behaviour, the key then being you can stop a behaviour from ever occurring by using the data/knowledge at hand. The best way to understand this is through a specific example, such as the one in Box 2.3.

---

### Box 2.3  An example of recognising antecedents to inform inclusion tactics

Sarah regularly refuses to do her work. She causes no real issues to other children and places her head on the desk during lessons when she does not want to work. Over the course of one term, Sarah's refusals to work or to follow instructions escalate from once per day to five times per day. Whilst this trend is concerning, the SENCO highlights the importance of uncovering the reason for the behaviour.

When first considering Sarah's situation, it may be misconstrued that she is just refusing to work and that it is a deliberate behavioural issue. The fact that the approach of using traditional rewards and sanctions has not worked indicates that there is something more going on. Therefore, it becomes even more important to look in-depth at any antecedents to the behaviour.

Upon closer inspection, some trends are discovered that relate to Monday mornings and to the end of the term. After speaking to the family, it is established that there have been changes at home over this period of time including a family friend and their children coming to stay, which has meant that Sarah has had broken sleep most nights.

With this new information, school staff are able to add strategies such as alerting sensory circuits, brain breaks and even a relaxation session for the child throughout the week to ensure that when she is in the classroom, she is ready and able to access the work.

### Reflection Questions

1. Are there any situations in which behaviour is not a communication of need?
2. To what extent does the behaviour policy in your school encourage teachers to consider antecedents?

---

It is helpful for schools to be explicit about how they support pupils within their behaviour policies. For example, here is an extract from the behaviour policy at a special school:

## Class teams can support our pupils by:

- Being curious about what children's behaviour may be communicating in the context of their experiences and needs.
- Being mindful and reflecting on the quality of our relationships with each other and them.
- Thinking proactively about the support and interventions we put in place to support them to learn self-regulation skills.
- By observing, gathering and analysing information – to ensure our interventions are personalised, well informed and planned according to the needs of each individual within the context of their class or within particular lessons on and off site.
- To work in class partnership with our pupils, their parents and carers, and other professionals working with them, so we are well-informed and have insight and understanding of a child's individual needs:. e.g., occupational therapy, speech and language therapy, cognitive behaviour therapy, CAMHS, etc.

- To invest time and allow safe spaces and opportunities for pupils to practice these skills and make mistakes from which they can learn, develop and grow.

Once teachers are more familiar with antecedents, they can share valuable insights with their pupils. These insights can help pupils to understand and to better communicate their needs whilst their behaviour and emotions are regulated. For example, a teacher might say something to a child, like 'when you put your head on the desk, you are communicating to me that . . .'. This type of interaction with children and young people can help them to learn how to communicate their needs without the need to include the challenging behaviour.

Returning to the ordinarily available provision in the classroom, school leaders should invest in long-term CPD programmes designed to support teachers to implement a universal design for learning. This might be thought of as inclusive practice that is vital for some pupils but valuable for all pupils. For example, if there are a small number of pupils with ADHD (Attention-Deficit Hyperactivity Disorder) who need movement breaks, this could be built into the lesson for all pupils rather than disrupting the flow of learning by providing something separate for those few pupils. Movement breaks are likely to welcomed by all pupils (how many children like sitting still for lengthy periods of time?), but building it into the learning process can improve the pedagogy too.

---

### Box 2.4  Building a movement break into the lesson

During a SEND learning walk in a secondary school, the SENCO observes a science lesson being taught by Mrs Hill. There are 29 pupils in the class, and three of them have needs which require the teacher to provide them with regular movement breaks.

One of the tasks the SENCO observes is Mrs Hill asking the class which scientist invented the telephone. She gives the class some possible options based on a recent homework task, including Elisha Gray, Antonio Meucci, Alexander Graham Bell or Johann Philipp Reis. As an aside, although Alexander Graham Bell is widely credited with this accolade, all four of these scientists arguably have a genuine claim to this accolade.

Around 12 pupils raise their hand hoping to be selected to respond to the teacher's question, but instead of choosing one pupil, she chooses four. Mrs Hill does not ask for the answer to her question but instead asks the four selected pupils to get out of their seats and for each of them to go a different one of the four corners in the room. Mrs Hill then announces that these four pupils are her 'four experts', and she asks every other pupil in the class to choose an expert. The pupils are required to get out of their seats and to go to the corner where their chosen expert is waiting. The four experts then briefed those in their corner about what they thought the correct answer was and why. Mrs Hill says that she will choose one pupil from each group (not one of the 'experts') to share the answer of their chosen expert and the reason why they have selected that particular scientist.

Later that day, the SENCO shares her feedback with the class teacher. She says that Mrs Hill's activity built a movement break into the lesson for all pupils (vital for some, valuable for all) and that the task was also good at maximising the participation of all pupils, not just those who raised their hands to respond to the question. Mrs Hill is delighted with the feedback and vows to undertake a similar activity in all her lessons going forwards.

### Reflection Questions

1. What are your reflections on Mrs Hill's approach to building a movement break into her science lesson?
2. Why does Mrs Hill think it is a good idea to build this same approach into all of her lessons going forwards? Do you think this is a good idea?
3. What feedback could the SENCO have given Mrs Hill about what she could have done differently to improve the experience of the pupils?
4. If movement breaks are provided as standard in lessons, then the three pupils who need this provision to meet their needs no longer require something that is 'different from or additional to' that which is available for all pupils. Therefore, should they still be included on the school's SEND register?
5. How else could Mrs Hill build movement breaks into her science lessons in a way that is also pedagogically better?

Another opportunity for implementing a 'vital for some, valuable for all' approach is to make assistive technology a tool that is available for all pupils as standard, not just those that require it to access the learning. Some examples of assistive technology that can be used for all pupils are the following:

- **Digital dictionaries.** These are typically used for pupils with dyslexia so they can quickly check the correct spelling of a word.
- **Google Translate paired with digital earbuds.** This low-cost solution is a useful way for pupils with EAL (English as an Additional Language) to receive a live translation of the teacher. Removing the EAL barrier can be helpful in identifying any underlying SEND.
- **Built-in accessibility tools.** Both Microsoft Office and Apple iPads have an extensive suite of accessibility tools available as standard. This includes coloured overlays, voice-to-text, text-to-voice and audio description. There is a setting that can be enabled in PowerPoint so that subtitles appear whilst the teacher is talking, with the option of live translation into multiple languages. The Siri tool on Apple was originally designed as an accessibility voice control feature for those unable to use their hands/fingers, but this is now widely used by many people.
- **AI (Artificial Intelligence).** Some schools are now using OpenAI and other generative AI tools in the classroom (explored further in Chapter 3). For example, if a teacher has children with a broad range of reading ages in their class, then AI can be used to generate alternative versions of the text that are accessible for those with different reading ages. Other schools are using AI tools to generate infographics that summarise complex content in a more immediately accessible format.

Getting back to the principle of 'vital for some, valuable for all', the SENCO at one secondary school explained how they believe a trauma-responsive approach benefits all pupils, not just those who have experienced recent or significant trauma. This fits with the views of the Headteacher at one special school, who added that whilst they build a trauma-responsive approach into their day-to-day practice, they do not talk about it explicitly because otherwise there is an assumption that it is only relevant for pupils who have experienced abuse or for looked-after children.

Returning once more to the ways in which schools can strategically build up their capability and capacity, several SENCOs suggest building up the list of trusted adults available as first responders for when pupils become dysregulated. In practical terms, SENCOs suggest drawing up a list of those pupils most likely to become dysregulated and considering for each of them which staff members they will respond well to. For those where there is only one first responder, there should be a proactive effort to build up the child's relationship with a second person over time, ensuring there is not a single point of failure or key person dependency.

Another strategy to be considered is for schools to introduce clinical supervision, which is a process of professional support that is often mandated for those working in health and social care settings. In some schools, clinical supervision might be targeted to provide support for specific staff, such as the SENCO and pastoral leads. However, it can also be used to support other front-facing staff who have regular interactions with children with a range of needs. For example, it could be the case that reception staff, site staff or learning support staff who experience verbal abuse from particular pupils would benefit from clinical supervision. In other schools, perhaps specialist settings, it might be more appropriate to provide clinical supervision for all staff. Sometimes there are local peer support models of clinical supervision available, but failing that, there are some national training providers such as the Centre for Inclusive Education at University College London.

---

### Box 2.5 Pre-mortems for identifying and mitigating risks

Many people have heard of a post-mortem, but relatively few have heard of a pre-mortem, which is its hypothetical opposite (Klein, 2007). In a medical context, a post-mortem is about understanding the reason why a person *has* died, so a pre-mortem would be about understanding in advance the reasons why a person *might* die. Transferring the concept of a pre-mortem into an education context for pupils with SEND, this would be about identifying in advance the things that could go seriously wrong when putting specialist provision in place. Very specifically, it is about identifying what could happen (the risks) that would make the provision fail completely.

Using a post-mortem in an educational context can be useful as it helps to understand why a particular provision has failed for a pupil, allowing any learning to be applied in the future for other pupils. However, such a post-mortem is of zero use to the pupil whose provision has already failed. This is where a pre-mortem comes into its own as it is a proactive process of identifying and mitigating risks.

From a practical perspective, a pre-mortem is about providing a safe space and a mechanism for all stakeholders to come up with the reasons why the planned specialist provision will fail. Once these reasons are identified, mitigating actions can be put into place, thereby increasing the chance of the provision being successful. Critics might argue that such risks should be identified routinely, but the reality is that this rarely happens. This might be because people do not want to put their head above the parapet by speaking truth to power or because those people with the necessary insights are not included. The pre-mortem exercise deliberately and unapologetically seeks out these risks.

For those who are new to the concept of a pre-mortem, next is an outline of the key steps. The entire pre-mortem exercise could be completed within under two hours.

1. **Stakeholder identification.** The person facilitating the pre-mortem should identify as many of the relevant stakeholders (including the family and the young person themselves) as possible to take part in the pre-mortem activity. However, there should also be an open invitation for others to put themselves forward to participate.
2. **Pre-mortem briefing.** The concept of a pre-mortem may be new, so the facilitator should explain what a pre-mortem is and why it is happening. The facilitator should also explain the needs and the planned provision for the pupil concerned.
3. **Generate reasons for failure.** As part of the session, those present should generate as many reasons for the provision failing as possible. The facilitator has a range of well-known tools available to them to support this process including mind-mapping, think-pair-share, de Bono's six thinking hats (focused on the black hat), starbursting or rapid ideation.
4. **Consolidation of reasons.** Once a range of reasons have been gathered, they need to be consolidated into key themes. Overlapping or contradictory reasons will need to be addressed so there is a consensus of understanding amongst the group about what the risks are.
5. **List the key risks and mitigations.** The key risks should be listed with appropriate mitigations and accountable owners identified in each case. This process can be supported by considering the causes of each risk, any leading indicators and any blind spots. It may be appropriate to use a RACI matrix (see Table 2.1) to map the role of different stakeholders for each of the mitigation actions.

A positive conclusion to the pre-mortem would be to ensure there is agreement on what the benefits of successful provision would yield. This is important because successful provision may not be the same as provision that delivers the intended benefits. For example, it is possible that provision consisting of a series of targeted interventions is delivered successfully but does not have the expected impact.

## Reflection Questions

1. How might parents/carers respond to being asked to be part of a pre-mortem exercise for their child? Is the medicalised and morbid terminology an issue?
2. Consider the statement, 'targeted interventions do not *go* wrong, they *start* wrong'. In your school, how much time is spent planning interventions to maximise their effectiveness?

Earlier in the chapter, a power and interest matrix was suggested as a tool for engaging stakeholders as part of the immediate response to a dysregulated pupil. This can also be used as a strategic tool for stakeholder engagement. Another strategic tool for mapping stakeholders is a RACI matrix, which is used to ensure there is a common understanding of the role of each stakeholder in relation to different tasks. RACI stands for 'Responsible, Accountable, Consulted (or Coproduced in this context), Informed. Table 2.1 shows an example of a RACI matrix related to some of the tasks associated with a targeted intervention for a pupil with SLCN. This is provided as an example of a RACI and is not intended to be a definitive list of the roles of all stakeholders. As a general rule, each task should only have one stakeholder who is accountable.

*Table 2.1* Example of a RACI matrix

| | Stakeholders | | | | | |
|---|---|---|---|---|---|---|
| Tasks | SENCO | SaLT | Teaching Assistant | Class Teacher | Pupil | Parents/ Carers |
| Accurately identify SEND | A | I | I | R | C | C |
| Secure and allocate the necessary resources | A/R | C | I | C | I | I |
| Ensure effective communication between home and school | A | I | | R | C | R |
| Deliver targeted intervention | A | R | | I | | I |
| Evaluate impact of targeted intervention | A | R | C | R | C | C |
| Monitor pupil progress over time | A | | | R | I | I |
| Update provision map | A/R | | | I | | I |

## The Duality of Behaviour Management and Parenting

There are a range of perspectives on the approach to behaviour management in schools. At one end of the spectrum, there are those who believe that strict, authoritarian, rules-based approaches work best. At the other end of the spectrum, there are those who believe that child-led approaches with limited, if any, use of discipline work best. In reality, both extremes are problematic, and the approach that works best is likely to be more pragmatic and responsive.

There is a duality between approaches to parenting and approaches to behaviour management, which may be useful for educators. The parenting approach balances the extent to which parents are responsive against the extent to which there are demands on, and expectations of, children, as shown in Figure 2.6.

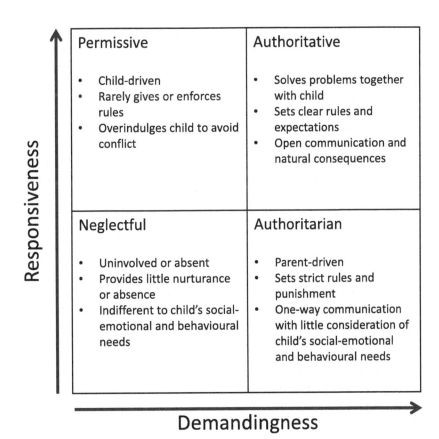

*Figure 2.6* The four parenting styles
*Source:* Zeltser (2021)

When adopting a trauma-responsive approach to parenting or behaviour management, there can often be a misconception that this is the 'permissive' approach. Furthermore, there is an illusion that being responsive means you are solely child-driven and that there are no rules or expectations for children. This is not the case. In practice, an effective trauma-responsive approach is 'authoritative' and is based on open dialogue and coproduced solutions.

Some feel that a trauma-responsive approach means that children have no boundaries, which in turn creates a lack of safety. Similarly, the adults may worry that they will have no control and are somehow at the will of the child. There may also be concerns about the scalability of a trauma-responsive approach as doing this for one or two children is very different to doing this for a whole class of children. Nevertheless, it can and does work, as has been demonstrated by Hope School in Liverpool.

## The 'Hope School' Approach

Hope School is an Ofsted outstanding educational provision in Liverpool for children with social, emotional and mental health needs. It is committed to providing exceptional quality education alongside compassionate and holistic care. At its heart, Hope is a safe, caring and enriching environment for the 68 children attending the school. It has built a formidable reputation, recognised as being a Centre of Excellence both locally and nationally.

As a specialist provision, the school supports children who can present with a complex range of needs which may include

- developmental difficulties,
- neurodiversity (including ASD and ADHD),
- learning difficulties,
- sensory processing difficulties,
- speech and language difficulties, and
- communication difficulties.

Hope School has consistently high proportions of pupils entitled to Pupil Premium and 'looked-after children' (59% and 18% respectively at the time of writing). Many of the children (and their families) have experienced adversity and trauma in their lives and may carry with them difficult experiences of relationships, both within and outside of school. Consequently, the school believes it is essential to address both the developmental and relational needs of all the children. The quality of relationships for the children and families is prioritised across all school activity with a particular focus on strengthening feelings of safety and trust. Staff at the school work hard to ensure that relationships across the school community are supported and nurtured.

Hope School has a team of 30 highly dedicated, motivated and specialist staff. The staff team understands that the children feel safer, more secure and ready to learn when their needs are well understood and addressed by the system of adults around them. Therefore, there is a commitment to strengthening psychologically responsive care at the whole school level with a focus on attachment- and trauma-informed practice. High quality CPD and supervision are provided for staff to enable them to address the needs of the children and, crucially, to support their families too.

Pupils can join the school at different times throughout the year and at different stages of their education between year one and year six. The pupils are predominantly from Liverpool Local Authority, although a small number attend from outside the area. Hope School also provides assessment places for pupils who are in the process of receiving an EHC plan but also at risk of permanent exclusion. A place at Hope School may be offered on a short-term basis for key stage one pupils.

The school strives to be a fully inclusive school and to ensure that all children are treated fairly and equally. Staff work in partnership with parents, carers and specialist partners to ensure pupils receive the appropriate support they need to access and to enjoy all aspects of school life. The school operates a non-exclusion policy, and they are exceptionally proud that since opening in 2002, no child has been excluded from the school.

Several years ago, after extensive research and a comprehensive strategic review, the school undertook a major change by removing its rewards and sanctions policy and embarked on a journey of implementing and developing attachment- and trauma-informed practices. This is not to be mistaken for a lack of rules and boundaries.

In practice, the school has clear systems of ensuring high standards and reinforcing positive behaviours. School leaders believe these create the sense of security and safety that children need to learn and to develop relationships with staff and with each other. Underpinning the school's approach is the notion that children need both clear boundaries and an adult that can remain open and connected to them when they need more time or support to reach expectations and live by the school rules.

The whole school *Attachment and Trauma Response Care Framework* is now well established in the school and underpins all the work undertaken with pupils, their families (parent/carers) and the wider school community. School leaders strongly believe this approach is transforming the lives of pupils so they have the skills and resilience to become lifelong learners.

> At the tender age of 12 my son has learnt who he is. He knows how to handle his emotions; he knows how to regulate himself; and he also knows what situations to avoid. He knows his limits, his triggers and he understands himself.
>
> (Parent of a former pupil at Hope School)

Hope School is now recognised both in Liverpool and at the national level for its attachment- and trauma-responsive approach. The school has a strategic partnership with Liverpool Virtual School, working in collaboration with clinical psychologists and other specialist partners to deliver a pioneering city-wide programme for schools across Liverpool aimed at strengthening attachment- and trauma-responsive care within education. Known as the HEARTS programme, it was named the 2023 gold award winner at the National Pearson Awards under the category of *Impact Through Partnership*. The school's involvement as a partner in such a prestigious and innovative project has undoubtedly been an honour for all concerned, and it reflects the reputation and respect given to the school by the wider education community.

Hope School has excellent internal and external facilities, including a full-size indoor climbing wall, an aerial hoop, several therapy rooms and two interactive sensory rooms. At its most recent two Ofsted inspections (November 2014 and April 2019), the school was graded as 'outstanding'.

---

### Box 2.6 Perceptions of SEND: superpower analogy

Imagine a world in which some people have the superpower of being able to fly. If only 2% of people have this ability to fly but you are part of the 98% that does not have this superpower, would you consider yourself to have a disability?

Having asked this question a lot to various audiences, the general consensus is that because the vast majority of people cannot fly, then the lack of this ability would be seen as 'typical' or 'normal' and would therefore not be considered to be a disability. Indeed, some people said they would consider those who could fly to be 'gifted' in some way as they are part of a small group of people who have an extraordinary talent or ability.

Now imagine a world in which 98% of people have the superpower of being able to fly, but you are in the 2% that cannot fly. Would you now consider yourself to have a disability?

Again, the general consensus from asking this question on multiple occasions is that this scenario is somewhat different to the first. If the vast majority of people can do something that they cannot do, many people said they would consider this to be a disability on their part.

Interestingly nothing has changed about your ability (or disability) to fly in each of these two scenarios. The only thing that has changed is the ability of those people around you and the wider operating environment. In the second scenario, the world is likely designed for the majority of people who can fly, so there may be supermarkets located in the sky that are now inaccessible to you.

The question is how best to address this disability or SEND. The medical model of disability advocates for 'fixing the individual'. In this context, it would involve targeted interventions that help you to learn how to fly or perhaps providing you with some sort of technological aid that gives you the power of flight. An alternative approach is the social model of disability, which advocates for 'fixing the environment' so that it is accessible to everybody irrespective of whether or not they can fly. Why build supermarkets in the sky when they could be built on the ground?

The social model demonstrates how getting it right for those with SEN or a disability will often work for all. It demonstrates that people can be included by removing barriers in the environment rather than requiring the individual to change. For example, having a lift in a building removes a barrier for somebody in a wheelchair, but it is also likely to be useful for other users of the building.

EQUALITY          EQUITY          LIBERATION

*Figure 2.7* Equality, equity and liberation

There are many variations of Figure 2.7 that were based on the original 2012 version by Craig Froehle, a business professor at the University of Cincinnati. The image is incredibly powerful in demonstrating the affordances and constraints of the different philosophies of inclusion.

Comparing the 'equality' image and the 'equity' image is useful, particularly if we imagine the three crates to represent bundles of additional support or resource that can be allocated to individual pupils with SEN or a disability. The 'equality' image shows that allocating resource equally for every pupil helps some to have access but does not help others enough. Indeed, it could be argued that some are receiving additional support that is unnecessary and at the expense of others who really needed a little more support.

Conversely, the 'equity' image shows a reallocation of the resource, resulting in everybody having a similar level of accessibility. Critics of this approach may argue that it is unfair to withhold additional resource from those who already have access since they have as much right as others to reach their own full potential.

Both the equity and equality images represent the medical model of SEND since they focus on 'fixing' the individual. However, the 'liberation' image is arguably a representation of the social model of SEN or disability since it demonstrates how removing a barrier to learning (exemplified by the fence), the overall environment is improved and there is accessibility for all pupils.

## Reflection Questions

1. When discussing a child's needs, do you use the medical terminology of 'diagnosis' or the social terminology of 'identification'? Does this align to your wider approach to provision in terms of the social model and the medical model?
2. What is the allocation of resources in your school when balancing the need to support the individual versus improving the accessibility of the environment?

Returning once more to the concept of ordinarily available provision, it is useful to think about this from a strategic perspective in relation to resource allocation. Figure 2.8 shows how the level of ordinarily available provision can influence the number of children that require special educational provision.

The blue areas in the diagram signify a 'rising tide', with a higher tide being a diagrammatical representation of a higher level of ordinarily available provision. The 'storm breakers' signify the needs of each pupil, with a higher storm breaker being a diagrammatical representation of a higher level of individual needs.

Phillipa Stobbs' (2023) rising tides concept shows that the higher the level of ordinarily available provision, the fewer the number of children that need special educational provision. However, a higher level of ordinarily available provision can also mean that the amount of specialist provision in place is too high in the context of the overall needs of the pupils as a group. In the diagram this is represented by the height of the tide above each of the storm breakers. It is therefore right to ensure the level of ordinarily available provision is appropriate for the volume and complexity of needs so that resources are deployed efficiently and effectively.

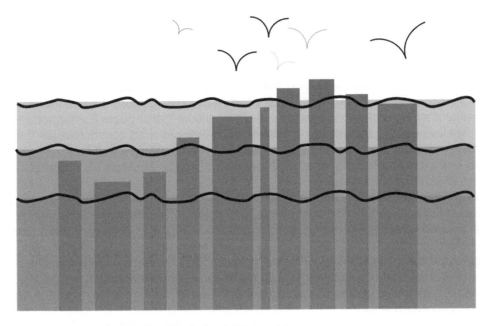

*Figure 2.8* Rising tides concept of ordinarily available provision
*Source:* Stobbs (2023)

## HEARTS

The Liverpool HEARTS framework has been devised in consultation with staff from the Liverpool Virtual School, key leads within the Liverpool Schools Project, Hope School in Liverpool, clinical psychologists from Changing Minds Child and Family Services (CMCAFS) and an education consultant.

HEARTS is an acronym for:

- **H**olistic Thinking
- **E**mpowering the School Community
- **A**spirations for All Pupils
- **R**elational Focus
- **T**rust and Safety
- **S**hared Purpose

The purpose of HEARTS is to combine the skills and expertise within Liverpool's education providers, teams and multi-agency partners, with the underlying evidence base around best practice to enable *all* pupils to thrive within education settings. The project focuses on how to provide high-quality, psychologically responsive care for everyone within the school community and to maximise the impact of this care so that it is beneficial for all staff and pupils. The project provides an opportunity to explore challenges and to establish the case for change, including why things might need to be done differently, particularly when thinking about how to best care for the most vulnerable children and young people.

The HEARTS delivery team work with key staff from each school on reflective conversations. They seek to strengthen what is going well and to find areas for development. They also provide guidance on how to change and improve school policies, processes and procedures as well as identifying emerging training needs. The approach is school-centred and absolutely not 'one size fits all'. The outcome is a community of schools with similar aims despite having significantly different starting points.

## Zero Exclusions

Hope School operates a zero-exclusion policy and has done so successfully for over two decades. The question is whether more schools can follow suit. The answer is that some already are and more can too. In the interests of sharing how this can practically be achieved, it is worth considering the strategies used by staff at Hope School. Here are some extracts from Hope School's Relational policy:

At Hope School we believe that:

- The quality of relationships (including strengthening feelings of safety and trust) throughout the school community are highly important and need to be supported and nurtured.
- Behaviour is a means of communication – we must ensure that all pupils are supported to communicate their needs safely and appropriately using their preferred communication systems.
- Fundamentally, our pupils are trying their best and want to behave well.
- Pupils feel safer and happier when their needs are well understood and addressed by the system of adults around them.
- When children feel safe in school, and have the opportunity to develop trusting relationships with adults who are attuned to their needs, and able to offer effective emotional and behavioural support, children will be more equipped to develop the skills they need to regulate themselves.
- We believe it is important that staff have a 'good enough' theoretical understanding of child's social and emotional development to help make sense of behaviour and needs. We want to ensure that staff have access to training, support and knowledge to develop and build their confidence and expertise.
- Pupils need a personalised approach to support them to manage their behaviour and consideration must be given to sensory and emotional needs, pain thresholds, what self-injurious behaviour could be communicating, levels of stimulation and engagement.
- As adults, we must consider the learning styles and needs of children and young people; we must also have realistic expectations about the rate of progress a pupil will make when learning to adapt or develop new behaviours.

These values and beliefs underpin the Hope School approach, but what happens when behaviour escalates? One framework used by staff at Hope School is the 'four Rs', as shown in Figure 2.9.

### Example of the Four Rs in Practice

Consider this scenario. A child turns up at school and shouts in a loud voice, "I hate it here". This scares other pupils as it was unexpected. The child then kicks a chair across the room, and luckily it does not hit anybody.

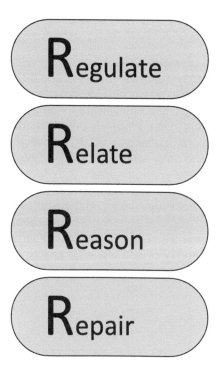

*Figure 2.9* The four Rs

The staff in the room have two immediate considerations. Firstly, the safety of those children in proximity to what is happening, and secondly the regulation of the child in question.

Following the 4 Rs approach, this could look something like the following:

- **Regulate.** Use presence, proximity and positive touch (if appropriate) to regulate the child. This can be followed up with deep pressure (this has a similar effect to a weighted jacket, but with a human connection) and some distraction questions about preferred topics in a calm and playful manner.
- **Relate.** Proactively notice the child's emotions and verbalise this. For example, "I can see by your face and what's happened that you're really angry today. I get angry sometimes too and it doesn't feel nice."
- **Reason.** Wonder out loud what may have happened this morning. This can be particularly successful when there is a strong existing relationship with the child or where there are good insights into the child's life. For example, "I wonder if you have left your swimming kit at home."
- **Repair.** There are two things that need to be repaired in this case: the issue for the child and the fear they created in the room. Using restorative questions, get the child to unpick who was impacted by their behaviour and, most importantly, how they could get help and support if a similar situation occurred again. This might be modelling scenarios that result in going to staff or leaving the swimming kit in school. The child could then repair the relationship with staff and pupils by writing an apology card or speaking to them. It is important that the apology acknowledges the impact of their behaviour on the rest of the class.

## *Zero Exclusion Strategies*

One interpretation of zero exclusion is that a child should be able to attend school all day, every day with no exceptions. This is a useful starting point and a laudable ambition, but sometimes there are circumstances where achieving an inclusive outcome in the long-term requires a more pragmatic approach in the short-term.

For example, consider the situation where a child needs access to specialist provision to have their needs met effectively and to be fully included. However, the finite capacity of specialist provision in the local area combined with where the pupil is on the priority list can mean the pupil remains in mainstream provision for a long time, despite this not being in their best interests. In such situations, some Headteachers have described how they felt that the only way to secure the required place in the specialist provision was to permanently exclude the pupil from their school. It seems counter-intuitive, but there was a clear view from multiple Headteachers that exclusion is sometimes necessary to achieve inclusion.

Another area of debate is the use of part-time timetables. Some argue this is a covert way of excluding pupils from school for large chunks of time without formally including them (Parkes, 2012). Some go further still, suggesting this is a way of disguising exclusion as inclusion (Graham et al., 2019, p. 51; Jones et al., 2003). However, there are also advocates of part-time timetables who argue that they are a useful strategy for avoiding a child being excluded in the first place. In particular, they cite the benefits of part-time timetables, including the following:

- **To support an effective induction.** Children need opportunities to be successful within the school's culture and ethos. Part-time timetables provide the opportunity for a child to make one mistake at a time and to learn from that. This is better than them making ten mistakes due to being in all of the time and then the whole situation being a write-off.
- **To build up trusting relationships.** Who can regulate a child on day one when nobody knows them yet? A part-time timetable allows time to build up quality, meaningful relationships.
- **To see the child in positive contexts.** Part-time timetables can support greater alignment between staff and pupil timetables, so that staff get the opportunity to know children in positive contexts, not only when they are in trouble. For example, the on-call person may only deal with the child when they are in bother, unless deliberate positive alternatives are put in place.
- **To break unhelpful behaviour cycles.** Changing habits is hard for anybody, so the opportunity to do this in small chunks and to have mini successes is important. Over time, the aggregation of marginal gain results in tangible progress.

It should not be underestimated how powerful a strong partnership between families and the school can be in contributing to effective SEND provision. However, it is too often the case that such relationships are steeped in tension and suspicion. Sometimes, the relationship can be challenging due to a specific incident, but in many instances there is likely a lack of understanding about why the other party is behaving in a particular way. For school-based staff seeking to develop strong relationships with parents or carers, a useful starting point is to reset any assumptions.

For example, SENCOs or teachers sometimes receive a narrative about a parent. They may hear that the parent is a 'persistent complainer' or a 'poor parent'. Such narratives do not have to be inherited and accepted. A better approach would be to ask the question, "What can I do to help?" After all, nobody wants to be a poor parent, so trying to understand what is happening and why may yield new options. This alternative approach avoids labelling parents and instead pushes the relationship towards coproduction and empowerment.

Another common assumption is that all parents understand from the outset what is expected of them. The headteacher in one school is aware that some parents struggle with reading, so in addition to any formal letters that go out, there is an accompanying text message that uses simple language. For example, the letter home about the pupils attending swimming lessons is accompanied by a text message, which simply states 'SWIM Thursday'. This Headteacher explains that by never assuming that parents can read, she avoids situations where they may be embarrassed.

Lastly, teachers should consider what experiences of school parents may have had themselves. This could have been in another country with different values and social norms, so their expectations of modern schooling in the UK are likely to be shaped by their own perceptions of school and of education more broadly.

## Red Lines – Stakeholder Perspectives

As was discussed earlier in this chapter, some Headteachers talk about having 'red lines', which, if crossed automatically, result in suspension or permanent exclusion. The notion of pre-determined red lines is problematic as it fails to take into consideration the contextual nature of any potential breach. Similarly, the purpose and benefit of such an exclusion may not always be clear.

There are certain behaviours that would generally be deemed as unacceptable, such as physical violence or illegal activity. These behaviours do need to be challenged and responded to, but the question is whether an automatic exclusion is always the most appropriate response.

For example, consider a situation where a pupil is bringing drugs into school. It may be appropriate to search the pupil on their way into school to avoid this, but once the drugs are taken away from the pupil and (if appropriate) reported to any necessary authorities, what is the benefit of denying the young person access to education by excluding them? If anything, the drugs indicate that the child is at risk within the local community, with any exclusion likely to give them extended access to drugs and to further normalise drug use at a young age.

The exclusion would likely be detrimental to the child and would not help to stop the drugs being brought into school. An alternative approach would be to look at how and why the child came into possession of the drugs in the first place. Similarly, what can be done to reduce the risk of this issue reoccurring, and how can the child's understanding of the impact of substance abuse be improved?

It is important to consider how any red line is being set and who it is for. In this example of drugs being brought into school, the flexibility of being able to move the red line allows the child to be kept safe and to continue to be educated.

When asked about the use of red lines and who benefits from excluding a child, there are four groups of potential beneficiaries that tend to be cited: the child, the school community, parents, staff. Each will now be considered in turn.

### The Child

A narrative that is often used is that an exclusion is in the interests of the child being excluded. For example, it might be argued that the child 'needs to learn to follow the rules' or that it is 'a fair punishment' for the behaviour itself.

Taking a step back, it is useful to consider how an exclusion feels to the child and what they actually experience. For some children, their parents/carers will take a harsh stance on exclusion, especially the first time. They may take away loved possessions from their child or make them work at home during the exclusion period. The intent of such an approach is for the child to remain up to date with the curriculum, but to deny them opportunities for interactions with peers and extra-curricular activities, thus making it an experience a child would not like to repeat. However, the reality is more likely to be that the child now feels alienated both at school and at home.

For other children, their parents/carers may not be in a position to take a harsh stance or may not agree with it. They might allow their child to play on computers or to play out in the local community during the period of exclusion. This less restrictive approach is ever more likely the more exclusions/suspensions occur.

Consequently, the child can end up perceiving this experience as rewarding the very behaviour trying to be reduced/eliminated. More worrying still is that a child out in the community may be vulnerable to grooming for things such as county lines. If the school community has been taken away, the child could end up looking for an alternative place to belong.

## The School Community

There are often concerns about the impact of undesirable behaviours on other pupils, their outcomes and the school community more broadly. An argument sometimes made is that one child or a small proportion of the school population is taking up a disproportionate amount of staff time, thereby reducing the opportunities for other members of the school community. These might be gifted and talented pupils, other pupils with SEND or other groups.

This raises important questions around the equitable distribution of resources. As a Headteacher or SENCO, there will be a continuous assessment of whether the current allocation of resources is sustainable or not. There will also be ethical questions to consider about whether resources are best deployed broadly across many pupils or targeted at fewer pupils. An exclusion may allow other pupils to improve their outcomes, but is this benefit to some pupils worth the cost to the individual child being excluded?

## Parents and Carers

There are two groups of parents/carers to be considered in this context. There are the parents of the child who has shown the undesirable behaviour, and there are the parents/carers of other children who are witnessing or being directly impacted by the undesirable behaviour.

For the parents of the child who is excluded, the impact may mean they are unable to work creating additional pressures in the home. Similarly, if the child is violent or controlling, this behaviour could be mirrored at home towards parents or siblings, putting further strains on family life. Over time, this could have a long-term impact on social care involvement.

The other group of parents may put pressure onto the school through complaints around safety and supervision for their child. Such demands can add to the time and workload pressures for senior staff and can be very complex to manage. An exclusion will likely appease this group of parents, but is this a sufficient rationale to warrant the exclusion?

## Staff

Given the current challenges of recruiting and retaining high-quality staff in schools, this stakeholder group is likely to be a high priority for Headteachers. Challenge and demands from staff are hard to ignore, especially when they are at the chalk face with the child and their parents on a daily basis.

It is important for staff to have clarity that exclusion is not an appropriate tool for providing respite and should only be used when there is a clear rationale for success and benefits realisation. This is a difficult balance to strike, but there are other measures that can support the approach. For example, the use of clinical supervision to support staff wellbeing can make a helpful contribution.

**Box 2.7  Primary school case studies**

Here are two examples of primary schools that have taken proactive action to reduce undesirable behaviours. Whilst reading about each school, it may be useful to consider what learning can be taken from their journeys and applied to your own context.

## Primary School A

This school made significant changes to their break time, having looked at data and realising that the number of incidents during football games at break time was too high. This was having a knock-on impact on the number of children missing lessons after break time.

The school decided to extend the break time into a longer, more structured play session. Football was removed as an option, and instead a number of outdoor play resources were introduced. The session was delivered collaboratively by all staff, including senior leaders. The children's voice helped to improve the sessions further still, and there was a significant reduction in issues after the session, but there were other benefits too. For example, there were improvements in communication and a reduced level of risk-taking.

The school has recently been inspected by Ofsted, and some of the comments were as follows:

- Pupils are happy and proud to belong to this calm and welcoming school community. They enthusiastically described many things that they appreciate about school, especially the friends that they make. Pupils benefit from caring and positive relationships with staff. They told inspectors that the school is a great place for them to learn.
- Pupils are polite and well mannered. They understand the importance of respecting others. They said that their school is a place where everybody is welcome. Pupils know that people should not be judged for any differences that they may have. Those pupils who have recently joined the school told inspectors that they have settled quickly in school. They value the many ways in which they have been helped to feel part of the school community.

One of the key learnings is that rather than preventing children taking part in outside play or football, the play can be changed to make it better meet the needs of pupils.

## Primary School B

This school decided that its use of the positive rewards behaviour system 'good to be green' was insufficient for their needs. The school transformed its approach and decided instead to use a psychologically informed behaviour policy. The policy advocates the use of

- emotional literacy,
- zones of regulation,
- opportunities for repair built in to lunchtimes,
- restorative conversations, and
- a therapeutic classroom set-up.

The change of approach in this school was challenging for some staff as they struggled without the 'good to be green' mechanism in the classroom. The school is clear that linking their strategy to research and using formulation to support teachers to become more reflective of their practice has enabled it to make rapid progress in this area.

This school has also been recently inspected, and here are a few comments:

- Pupils are exceptionally polite and courteous. They conduct themselves impeccably well in lessons and around the school. They are highly considerate of each other's right to a calm environment, which means that disruptions to the school day are very rare.
- They spoke to inspectors with passion and empathy about the importance of mental wellbeing. Pupils seek out opportunities to help each other wherever they can. They learn how to develop safe and healthy relationships.

## The 'Nisai Approach' to Respond to School Exclusion (by Laura Brown, Nisai Group)

Nisai Group was founded in 1996 to provide a personalised and flexible education system to those learners who were unable to engage with a mainstream education. This online teaching platform would supply the best parts of a school whilst allowing for any required adaptations. Live teaching ensures that all learners are getting the appropriate support and immediate feedback that will allow for progression. The online classroom provides anonymity for those that require it and alternative communication methods which help to meet learner needs.

Nisai Group supports learners across key stages three, four and five, with additional learners up to the age of 25 in receipt of an EHC plan. This allows learners to follow a stable education and progress onto their chosen career pathways or to enter further education. In essence, Nisai allows traditional and non-traditional learners, both in and outside of the UK, to achieve their goals whilst developing new skills and passions. Nisai is focused on providing quality education to all and removing barriers that would otherwise limit their final outcomes.

Young people across the UK and the wider world have faced a lot of upheaval in recent years. The Covid-19 pandemic, the growth of social media as well as ever-changing government policy means that the stability that many crave has not been available. This has led to a limitation of their engagement and a dip within projected outcomes. This has been widely accepted as something that needs to be worked on to be able to support these young people back to their anticipated levels of progression.

Now consider this same situation for learners with SEND, who may rely more on routine and structure. These learners may have more complex needs and a broader range of professionals who support them. These learners may also struggle more with change or engaging with social 'norms'. This group of young people will face more difficulties in being able to reach their full potential or to engage in the same type of activities as their peers, which can lead to overall exclusion.

Exclusion can be broken down into two broad areas: academic exclusion and social exclusion. Each of these will come with their own difficulties and lasting results for learners with SEND.

### Academic Exclusion

Academic exclusion amongst learners with SEND is disproportionately high.

> In autumn term 2022/23, there were 3,100 permanent exclusions. This is an increase from 2,100 in autumn 2021/22 but is still slightly lower than the final pre-pandemic autumn term (2019/20) when there were 3,200 permanent exclusions.
>
> (DfE, 2023b)

For almost 50% of these exclusions to be of learners with SEND (either with or without a statement or EHC) shows that there is an underlying issue that needs to be dealt with. Learners with SEND make up only 17% of the overall learner cohort. The comparison of these figures pre- and post-pandemic shows that this is an ongoing issue rather than something that has stemmed from the pandemic.

Training staff to understand the needs of the learners and ways to support SEND is vital, showing that the behaviour of these learners may be due to other factors rather than deliberate misbehaviour.

> Persistent disruptive behaviour was included as a reason in 55% of all suspensions and 49% of all permanent exclusions in autumn term 2022/23.
>
> (DfE, 2023b)

The education of these learners is being disrupted through exclusion. They are missing out on the opportunity to pick up vital knowledge and to follow societal interaction with their peers, based on a number of factors which may be out of their control. A system that would encourage their engagement should be introduced as a priority, rather than excluding them.

Academic results can be affected by this missed education and the inequalities of the mainstream education system for these learners. A comparison between SEND learners and non-SEND learners shows that average Attainment 8 scores are consistently lower for those with SEND. From a maximum score of 90, non-SEND learners have an average score of 52.5. Those learners with SEN support in place without an EHC Plan see this figure fall to an average of 34.9, and those with an EHC plan will see it drop further to 14 (DfE, 2023c). This average score will cause a ripple effect across the future of the learner and the employment that they can expect to go on to.

## Social Exclusion

Social exclusion can be just as important for learners with SEND with respect to learning social cues and expectations, as well as providing suitable levels of interaction to allow for a strong level of mental health and wellbeing.

> Socially excluded students are at higher risk of experiencing increased negative academic and social outcomes, such as early school dropout, criminality and depression.
>
> (Leeuw et al., 2018)

According to Article 23 of the United Nations *Convention on the Rights of the Child*, we should 'recognise that a mentally or physically disabled child should enjoy a full and decent life in conditions which ensure dignity, promote self-reliance and facilitate the child's active participation in the community' (United Nations, 1989). School exclusion can limit this 'active participation' and therefore limit the inclusion levels of all learners.

> Advocates of inclusive education argue that the development and potential of students with SEN improve when they are educated with typically developing (TD) peers because they are afforded more social opportunities.
>
> (Leeuw et al., 2018)

Using an inclusion room can segregate these learners due to them receiving only part of the social interaction that other learners receive.

> Segregation of children with special needs, permanent exclusion of unruly and difficult children, and, to some degree, differentiated schooling structures can foster social exclusion, particularly if they are primarily aimed at freeing the regular school system from poorer achievers and more difficult students rather than cater specifically to their needs.
>
> (Klasen, 2001)

The needs of the learner in the inclusion room are often not at the centre of the decision to place them there. Instead, they are typically there so that they do not disrupt the learning of others. Suitable alternatives are too often not put in place for the segregated learner. Schools will continue to follow their policies, which arguably do not meet the needs of those learners, with an alternative to a mainstream education possibly being required in this situation.

> The impact of such educational outcomes is to exclude children from the benefits of education and the citizenship rights and the opportunities it opens up. It also contributes to social exclusion as adults through the nexus of educational outcomes and unemployment, poverty, and neighbourhood dynamics.
>
> (Klasen, 2001)

Social exclusion can also take place when differentiation is included to support learner needs.

> Peers named the presence of teacher assistants who spend time with students with SEN as well as dependence on parents (e.g., the necessity to accompany to e.g., leisure activities) as a barrier of inclusion.
>
> (Lindner et al., 2022)

Any difference will be recognised by young people and will add a level of awkwardness to interaction. If an SEN learner has a teaching assistant with them, then a TD learner might feel that they are unable to converse with them both at the same time. If an SEN learner's parents are present, then a TD learner might not be able to act in the same way around them as they can with the other learners.

> Peers' lack of knowledge in alternative communication skills and their friends influence towards students with SEN were discussed as additional barriers in building relationships with students with SEN.
>
> (Lindner et al., 2022)

Again, separating the SEN learner to be able to support their needs means that the mainstream system for the TD learners remains in place. Time is not typically spent educating the TD learners as to how they can engage with the SEN learners in other ways, leading to further social exclusion.

## Equality and Equity

Equality in education means that all learners receive the same thing. This relates largely to the same standard of education and having equal access to the same provision. Equality, diversity and inclusion (EDI) is a common focus within education. This will build a healthy environment that is welcoming and supportive. This atmosphere is pivotal for allowing further growth and building lifelong learners. Inequality can build lifelong barriers or defences within the young people and cause further problems with regards to outcomes or their confidence and self-esteem.

This level of equality provides us with the mainstream schooling system. Without a doubt this system has been suitable and successful for millions of young people for over 50 years. They have been able to benefit from high standards, appropriate resourcing and free access. It has been maintained through observational bodies such as Ofsted and regulators such as JCQ. No longer did learners have to pay for education or pass an entrance exam to be given the opportunity to reach their potential at a school with higher standards. All schools are required to meet these standards and the league tables will compare the outcomes of this.

Schools are aiming to be the best that they can be and to ensure there is equality. Equality allows learners from different backgrounds to access the same educational provision and so they also learn from each other. They can mix with peers from different cultural or socio-economic backgrounds. This removes some barriers and allows the learners to progress further in the workplace following on from their schooling as they are able to communicate with a variety of peers.

Educational equality tries to remove class barriers by affording the same opportunities to working-class and middle-class learners. Although there continues to be a gap in outcomes between these classes both groups have improved and have achieved more than they would have done without this equality.

Currently, equality is a key focus in inclusive education. The provision of the same thing for all learners. At first sight, this is a good thing. Providing the same thing for all learners is surely fair? But if we all have different needs then this is not always true. Nisai Group favours the approach of educational equity. This model understands that the individual needs of the learner mean that there is still the requirement for some adaptation and differentiation in order to provide a truly supportive environment for all.

Some of the behavioural issues that lead to exclusion from schools are not due to the learner misbehaving, but due to the school's response to behaviour which stems from SEND. Nisai allows for learners from multiple backgrounds to come together and to benefit from more focus and individuality than may be available in a mainstream setting due to the expectations that are placed on them. Nisai is able to teach smaller groups at one time, taking into account the duration of a session in line with the ability to focus on their learning and place learners in groups based on their ability rather than their age and the government expectations at that time.

Nisai recognises that some learners have gaps which need filling before moving them to their age expected study. These stages are all beneficial to learners as the focus can then be placed on the learning, in a way which suits them. This leads to higher levels of engagement, fewer behavioural issues and better outcomes.

Equity recognises that one-size does not always fit all and that each learner will require different levels of support at different points of their education. Being able to adapt and change in line with this will provide the learners with the same opportunities as their TD peers.

The Nisai model provides equality as it is available to all learners, not only those with SEND. SEND and TD learners will be placed alongside each other with no awareness of the background of each other. They will communicate and react to each other with no prejudice or awkwardness. Each individual has the opportunity to develop their own skills and to recognise the positives of each situation.

Equity at Nisai allows the learners to be in charge of their own decisions around communication. There is often concern regarding social interaction through online learning and providing the ability for inclusion in this area. The lessons are delivered live with teachers and learners logged in together. They are able to engage with their lessons and their peers in real time and build relationships as if they were in a physical classroom, with some of the additional barriers removed. They are able to talk privately to the teacher if this is their preferred style, and yet they can see the interactions between the other students. This allows them to build on their social skills and mirror the actions of their peers. They can communicate with peers outside of lessons, using the groups and clubs based around their favourite hobbies. These allow learners to converse with peers with similar interests which helps them to learn how to build a conversation and maintain suitable levels of communication across these. Staff members will support in these areas, as well as there being opportunities for additional sessions which focus on the development of skills outside the academic arena.

The majority of learners referred to Nisai have some elements of SEND as shown in Figure 2.10. The teachers at Nisai have a specific knowledge of the needs of each learner and the methods that have worked for them in the past as well as those that have been detrimental to their progression. This means that there is greater scope for individualisation within delivery and for real inclusion to be experienced. Teaching will adapt and change depending on the cohort of each group of learners. This system has been very effective over almost 30 years of experience, with the results from the 2022/23 academic year being the best to date with GCSE and A Level pass rates of 99% and 96% respectively. This goes against the national trend of a dip in results during this year. These results signify higher rates of achievement than were expected of them during their time in mainstream schools, especially for those learners with SEND.

The application of an equitable educational provision allows for the continued mobility of learners at Nisai, building to liberation for many (see Figure 2.7). Some learners may not achieve the nationally expected number of GCSEs or all of these at the higher grades. However, the progression that they make and the opportunities that open up due to this provision allows further opportunities outside the classroom, including a greater equality of employment opportunities.

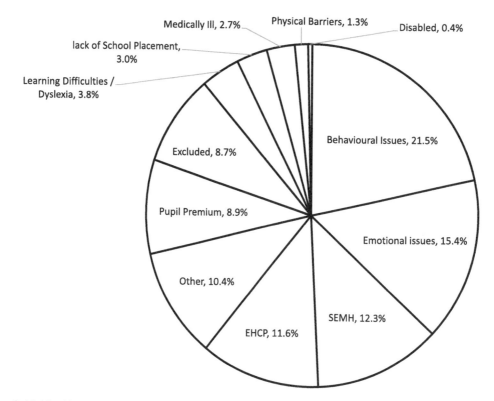

*Figure 2.10* Nisai breakdown of needs (2022/2023)

During the 2022/23 academic year, Nisai learners were able to continue their educational journey. Many were able to continue with Nisai into the 2023/24 academic year with an increase to their academic level, there were also a variety of other destinations which opened up to them.

The destination of learners shows how they have been able to engage with their provision and the way that this has potentially changed their future opportunities. On the basis of the data that is shared with Nisai, over 80% of learners from the 2022/23 academic year were able to move on to further education at university, at college or through reintegration with their mainstream provision. This opens the door for them to be able to achieve their outcomes with qualifications that they had not previously been prepared for achieving.

6% of learners went straight into employment or apprenticeships following the completion of their course. This builds their social mobility and allows them the opportunity to develop appropriate skills for the workplace. As part of this they will be exposed to other aspects of life and will learn social skills from people with a variety of backgrounds. This will help them to continue their personal development as lifelong learners and enable them to gain a footing within their community.

Through the opportunity to access an educational provision which focuses on equity, these learners have far surpassed their previous expectations, and these outcomes have allowed them to reach destinations which have previously been unavailable to them and a large number of other learners with SEND currently struggling within a mainstream school or those that have been excluded based on the behaviours that they are showing.

Learners who have been able to reach their potential after studying with Nisai have recognised the support that they received. A number of learners have maintained contact with Nisai and provide regular updates on their continued progress. These learners have engaged in some fantastic experiences, completing university studies and entering their chosen career path or successfully applying for apprenticeship positions and moving on to higher roles within this area.

However, grades are not the only way to measure progress and success. Many learners have achieved personal goals through their engagement. Remote education has provided the opportunity to some to travel across the world and compete in competitive sport competitions whilst maintaining consistency with their education. Others have been unable to leave their house, and yet with support they are completing social activities and expanding their horizons. Others still have passed a driving test that they thought was beyond them, with additional support in literacy to be able to complete the theory test. Equity in this sense has truly provided liberation for these learners with increased social mobility due to their achievements.

> While all countries are aiming to progressively integrate children with special needs, in some countries, including the Czech Republic, Hungary, and Switzerland, physically and mentally disabled children as well as children with learning difficulties are still largely taught in separate school systems. . . . Since there typically is very little upward mobility out of such school systems into the regular education, being placed in such a separate school system can become a form of social exclusion.
>
> (Klasen, 2001)

Nisai as a provision allows learners to receive an education in a style which suits them to achieve their goals. Some will use this to complete their qualifications, continue onto further education, apprenticeships and university provision in line with their TD peers. Others will use it to fill in gaps and return to a mainstream provision with more awareness of methods that are beneficial to them, abilities to work in line with the expectations for their age range and a knowledge of alternatives that they can expect to be supported with in the future. This allows for onward mobility and social liberation. They will be able to continue to a place where they can follow their aspirations and be free of additional barriers or constraints.

## Conclusion

This chapter has explored the national data related to school exclusions, which shows that there are too many exclusions and that pupils with SEND are disproportionately excluded. To address this issue, it is recommended that Headteachers avoid having arbitrary 'red lines' and that there is a concerted effort to ensure that coproduction is effective. Where there are issues around undesirable behaviours, staff should use strategies that focus on 'connection before correction', as exemplified by the approaches of both Hope School and Nisai. Ultimately, the priority should be to identify and implement solutions rather than to attribute blame.

## Reflection Questions

1. To what extent do the behaviour and exclusion policies in your school align with the school's wider commitments to diversity, equity, inclusion and belonging (DEIB)?
2. What trends can be observed in your school's exclusions data? Based on this, how could the school adjust its approach to behaviour and inclusion to reduce the need for exclusions?

## Suggested Resources

1. The *School Exclusions video guide for caregivers* is a government-funded resource designed to provide an overview of school's exclusions for parents, carers and guardians. It focuses on how to prevent exclusions, alternatives to exclusion, and what to do if exclusions do occur. It discusses how to get help and legal advice as well as how to identify and respond to unlawful exclusions.
www.wholeschoolsend.org.uk/news/school-exclusions-video-guide-care-givers
2. The *School Exclusions Hub* provides free information and resources for professionals and community organisations supporting children and their families to challenge school exclusion. It is part of *Coram Children's Legal Centre*.
https://schoolexclusionshub.org.uk/

# 3   Data for Delivery

We live in a world that is increasingly data rich (Savva, 2020), and our education system is no exception. The activities of monitoring, recording and reporting create data and insights that can be used to inform priorities and decision-making in schools.

It is common for schools to have somebody who is responsible for data. In larger settings, there might be a role specifically for this purpose, such as a Data and Insights Officer. However, many schools do not have the luxury of such a post, and so the responsibility forms part of somebody's wider role. This could be an administrator who is experienced with data (the school's timetabling officer is a popular choice), or perhaps an Assistant Headteacher or Deputy Headteacher who has 'data' as part of their remit.

For routine data analysis, this approach works well and can reduce the workload of teachers, allowing them to focus on tasks that better lend themselves to their educational expertise. However, if all data-related tasks are completely separated from the educationalists with first-hand knowledge of the individual children, there is a risk of overlooking data that could yield important insights. This is particularly true when it comes to pupils with SEND since some of the more routine data analyses may be less relevant without further refinement. For example, a pupil who is regularly not attending school due to their needs may benefit from a more nuanced approach to reporting their attendance rates. A similar argument could be made for pupils with moderate learning difficulties, where a more nuanced approach to reporting their progress data is needed. The SENCO is a person of strategic influence who understands the individual pupils and their needs, so they are well placed to inform such approaches. However, it may also be necessary for the person responsible for data to consider how such individual cases might skew cohort-wide data.

The point here is that it is beneficial for SENCOs to be able to interrogate data directly when it comes to pupils with SEND. They are uniquely placed to identify insights for individuals and for groups of pupils with similar needs by combining their SEND experience and expertise with the available data sets. For clarity, this is not an argument that SENCOs should be doing all data analysis when it comes to pupils with SEND, but rather that they should be able to complement and shape routine data analysis. So the SENCO's work on data is in addition to, not instead of, routine data analysis. Another way of expressing this expectation is that SENCOs do not need to be data analysts, but they do need to be data literate.

Data literacy for SENCOs could be thought of as 'the ability to understand, interpret and effectively use data to inform practices and decision making' (Howieson et al., p. 149). When SENCOs develop their data literacy, they can draw on more data sources and richer data sets, allowing them to gain a more holistic understanding of individuals and groups of pupils with SEND.

During the interviews and conversations with SENCOs for this book, it quickly became clear that whilst many of them understood the importance of data, very few had sufficient self-confidence in their capability to optimise their use of data. Variations of the following four quotes were raised by multiple SENCOs:

> I hate using Excel. I much prefer somebody giving me the table of data in Microsoft Word, so I can just copy and paste it into whatever report I need to write.

> I understand children, but I'm terrible with numbers. I have always been bad at maths.

> Data is not part of my job as a SENCO. It's like you wouldn't go to your doctor for help with your times tables, so why ask a SEND professional for help with data.

> I'm okay with data, but I worry about getting something wrong. What if somebody who knows what they're talking about challenges me? I'm scared I will be found out. Maybe it's imposter syndrome or maybe other people should worry about the data side of things?

These quotes provide a useful sense of SENCOs' perspectives of their own capabilities as well as their view that there is a lack of a justification for them needing to analyse data directly.

DOI: 10.4324/9781032634807-3

However, despite such frequent comments from SENCOs, it is interesting that when pressed further, SENCOs often talked at length about many different ways in which they use data. This suggests that there is a gap between SENCOs' confidence, their perceptions and the practical reality.

As an aside, the comments from multiple SENCOs about being 'bad at maths' echo similar sentiments to what might be heard in wider society. It is interesting that it is socially more acceptable to share that you struggle with numeracy than it is to say that you struggle with literacy. As a specific example, it is generally the case that at a gathering of friends, an individual might (unfairly) feel embarrassed or ashamed to admit that they struggle with reading, whereas admitting that they struggle with adding up is more likely to be echoed by others. This mismatch of ideals is perhaps more problematic when it comes from educators as there is an implicit expectation that they should give an equivalent status to both numeracy and literacy.

Ultimately, this chapter seeks to explore the ways in which SENCOs typically use data in their role, including how to find and use SEND-specific government data sets that are readily available in the public domain. Given the dominance of Office 365 within schools, a step-by-step guide will be provided for the top five features of Microsoft Excel that SENCOs need to use most regularly.

For SENCOs who are lacking confidence, experience or expertise in using data, the chapter includes practical ideas for improving data literacy and becoming more data-savvy. The ethical issues of 'watermelon reporting' and 'strategic misrepresentation' are discussed, and greater clarity is given to the reliability and validity challenges of using SEND cohort data when individual pupils can have such diverse needs.

The chapter concludes with some practical advice on how to advance the strategic reporting in schools through improved prioritisation about *what* data is reported and improved communication in *how* that data is reported. Given the rapid acceleration of artificial intelligence (AI) into everyday usage in society, some reflections are provided on the opportunities and implications of this technology for SENCOs, SEND provision and for schools more broadly.

## Typical Data Usage by SENCOs

During the interviews and conversations, SENCOs shared many ways in which they use data. The starting point was often a statement by SENCOs that they do not use data as much as they should do because, as one SENCO put it, 'I am not a data-person'. However, such statements were often followed up by many ways in which they did use data. The 'top five' self-reported uses of data by SENCOs ranked from most common to least common:

1.  **The demographic profile of pupils on the SEND register.** This includes the overall numbers and proportions of pupils with SEND, broken down by those at SEN Support (sometimes referred to as 'SEN K') and those with EHC plans. It is also common for SENCOs to keep a 'watch list' of pupils who may have SEND or those who have recently been removed from the SEND register.
2.  **The progress and attainment of pupils with SEND compared to pupils without SEND.** In many instances, comparisons are made to the equivalent regional or national data. A small number of SENCOs raised concerns about progress and attainment data for pupils with SEND being used to sit alongside (but not within) a set of 'shadow data', which consists of the progress and attainment of pupils *without* SEND. Such shadow data is being compared to regional or national data, which includes all pupils. SENCOs understandably feel that this is an unfair comparison and that it suggests that pupils with SEND are a barrier to meeting external expectations of progress and attainment.
3.  **The number of pupils with SEND who have been excluded.** SENCOs are familiar with the number of pupils with SEND who have been excluded from school, either fixed term or permanently. SENCOs reported that they are commonly asked to provide data on the overall numbers of pupils with SEND excluded as well as contextual data about individual cases. However, when pressed further about the prevalence of exclusions and how this compares to other schools, there was far more variability in SENCOs' responses. Many were unsure whether their school's exclusion rate for pupils with SEND was above, below or in line with what was happening in other schools in the areas or with regional or national averages.

4. **Attendance rates for pupils with SEND.** More than half of SENCOs commented that they routinely monitor or receive attendance rates (or absence rates) for all pupils on their SEND register. However, when asked about what constituted 'good attendance', there was no consistent expectation amongst SENCOs. Some SENCOs reported that expectations were determined on an individual basis, noting, for example, that pupils with medical needs or those who are school refusers may spend a disproportionate amount of time away from school. Other SENCOs felt it was not their place to determine what constitutes 'good attendance'. More generally, even amongst SENCOs who regularly report on attendance data, there is debate and confusion about which codes should be used to record different types of absences.

5. **Prevalence of primary areas of need.** SENCOs reported routinely updating their SEND register and or provision map to reflect the prevalence of different types of SEND, such as autism, hearing impairments or moderate learning difficulties. The SEND categories used by SENCOs are generally aligned to those used for national data collection as part of the January census. However, it is also common for SENCOs to supplement these categories with other needs they feel are not sufficiently represented within the January census primary areas of need. For example, attachment needs and eating disorders are often added by SENCOs. Whilst less common, some SENCOs had *Fragile X* or *Foetal Alcohol Syndrome* listed as additional primary areas of need.

Whilst the prevalence of primary areas of need is data often collated by SENCOs, very few said that they benchmarked this data against regional or national data. The other common area of SENCO uncertainty in recording this data was how to categorise pupils who are on a formal identification pathway. For example, one SENCO described how she was '99% sure that [a pupil] has ADHD', and she explained that the pupil was on the neurodevelopmental pathway via the local authority to be formally assessed with the aim of securing a diagnosis. In the absence of a formal diagnosis, the SENCO remains unsure about how to record such data. SENCOs are generally frustrated that national guidance on making such judgements is not readily available.

Beyond this top-five uses of data, plenty of other data usage was reported by SENCOs. In addition to the primary areas of need, SENCOs shared that they are increasingly using the four broad areas of need from the SEND Code of Practice (DfE and DoH, 2015) to break down other data sets, such as attendance, exclusions and progress. Their intention is to identify patterns that can help them to be more effective in targeting their resources. For example, if exclusions are higher for pupils with SEMH needs than for the other broad areas of needs, then the SENCO can explore removing barriers or introducing early interventions for this specific group of pupils.

Lots of the SENCOs interviewed commented that they pay particular attention to pupils with SEND who are also looked after (LAC) or disadvantaged (eligible for Pupil Premium) when reporting data. In a few cases, the SENCOs noted that they are formally required to use data to provide insights on pupils based on more complex intersectionality. However, for most of the SENCOs, such reporting is not an expectation, but rather something they choose to do because they believe it adds value and aids understanding.

Another common use of data reported by SENCOs is to populate reports for governors or to prepare for Ofsted inspections. This typically consists of a combination of both quantitative and qualitative data. The quantitative data is largely captured by the 'top five' list earlier. The qualitative data tends to be focused on individual pupils or small groups of pupils, such as those participating in a particular intervention. Pen portraits, case studies and impact reports are regularly used by SENCOs for such purposes.

## Conspicuous Omissions

Before looking at some of the alternative uses of data by SENCOs, it is perhaps timely to reflect on a few of the observations that it was anticipated SENCOs might have included but that were conspicuous by their absence or at best only peripheral remarks.

Firstly, the notion of using quantitative data to benchmark against tailored success criteria for individuals or for small groups of pupils was rarely discussed. For example, consider the case of an individual child with SEND in a primary school who is not expected to meet age-related expectations (ARE) nor are they expected to achieve the same levels of progress as other pupils in their class. Only one SENCO commented that they regularly shared with senior staff whether or not individual pupils with SEND had achieved their individual expected progress as a part of routine data reporting.

Similarly, there was only one SENCO who talked about regularly reporting to the Headteacher and governors on the proportion of pupils who were on track to meet their individual targets as set out in their EHC plans. These targets are personalised and made up from both qualitative and quantitative data. Therefore, the rationale from the SENCO concerned was that 'there is no reason this figure should not be 100% assuming we have been given the resources to put the necessary provision in place'. This particular SENCO was also mindful about placing too much emphasis solely on academic attainment data, favouring a more holistic approach to reviewing outcomes data. Very specifically, she argued that it was more important for children to grow up able to 'operate independently and effectively as part of wider society than to have great exam results.' When pressed further on academic progress, the SENCO pointed out that 'progress is also not linear' and that we should be concerned with 'helping children to achieve when they are ready, rather than when we think they should be ready'.

The notion of differentiating between outcomes and benefits is useful from an educational perspective. In this context, an outcome can be thought of as *what* has been achieved, whilst a benefit is more about the purpose and *why* it needed to be achieved. For example, a targeted literacy intervention may deliver the outcome that a child has improved reading. However, it should be assumed that this outcome will automatically deliver the intended benefits. The purpose of helping the child to improve their reading may have been to help them be more independent in lessons and not so reliant on additional support. There may need to be a specific effort to use the outcome in order to realise the benefits. The one school leader who talked about this suggested that whilst SENCOs and their teams may deliver outcomes, it is teachers in classrooms every day who realise the benefits.

There is a Dutch expression about a surgeon that is sometimes used to emphasise this distinction between outcomes and benefits. It makes that point that just because a successful outcome has been achieved, it does not mean that the benefits have been realised.

The operation was successful. The patient is dead.

## Further Ideas for Data Usage by SENCOs

### *SEND Identification Data*

Around July each year, the Department for Education publishes SEND identification data for every school in the country on its website (DfE, 2023d). This data is based on the January census, and it also contains regional and national data, which can be used for benchmarking. The six-month time lapse between January and July means the data is often not accessed until the autumn term. This means it will be based on the school cohort of the previous academic year, which must be taken into account if using this data. The Department for Education website also includes historic data for every January census going back to 2010, which is useful for mapping trends over time.

To access the school-level data for a particular year, the 'download all data' zip-file should be used. Once the file is downloaded onto the computer, the folder called 'supporting files' or 'ancillary' should be opened. Inside this folder is a spreadsheet called 'SEN school level underlying data' or 'SEN school level UD'. This is the spreadsheet that contains the identification data for every school in the country.

Once the spreadsheet is opened, it can be overwhelming as it contains more than 24,000 rows of data. This is because each row represents an individual school/setting. There are many ways to find the row for a particular school, such as using its unique reference number (URN) if you know it, but perhaps the simplest way is to use the 'filter' function (see the 'Basics of Excel' section for further guidance). Filter first for the local authority of the school you are looking for, then for the name of the school. This will leave one row representing one school. Some of the entries in this row include SEND identification data. In addition to the total number of pupils at the school, there is an entry for the total number of pupils with EHC plans and the total number of pupils at SEN support. For both EHC plans and SEN support, there is a breakdown by the 'primary area of need'. This data can be used to create the following:

- The proportion of pupils at the school with SEND
- The proportion of pupils at the school at SEN support
- The proportion of pupils at the school with EHC plans
- The proportion of pupils with SEND that have particular primary areas of need

By repeating this exercise for different academic years, it is possible to see how these proportions have changed over time and to create trend data.

The equivalent data for all pupils in a local authority or for all pupils nationally can be obtained in the same way from grouped data within the spreadsheet. However, other spreadsheets within the downloaded folder also contain this data, and it is helpfully broken down by phase as well as pupil characteristics, including age, gender, ethnicity, free school meals and year group. Phase specific, regional and national data can be used as a benchmark for individual schools.

For clarity, there is no expectation that the proportion of learners with SEND in any individual school should mirror local or national averages. However, where there are significant variations, it is useful to understand why this might be the case. Table 3.1 considers three common scenarios where this data might highlight variation from the benchmark and provides some possible reflection questions.

Table 3.1 is focused on benchmarks related to the total proportion of pupils with EHC plans or at SEN support. When it comes to benchmarking against the proportion of pupils with SEND for each of the primary areas of need, a more nuanced approach is required. To get an idea of how this might work in practice, Table 3.2 and Figure 3.1 set out a fictitious example of how a school from Blackpool, Lady Videtta High School, might use a particular set of published census data.

Table 3.2 shows the total proportion of pupils with SEND for each primary area of need compared to the equivalent regional and national data. Figure 3.1 shows the same data as a comparative bar chart. It should be noted that this data is fictional and purely for the purposes of demonstrating how this type of data can be used to inform strategic decision-making. Here are some questions that the SENCO or other strategic leaders at the school may wish to consider in relation to this particular set of data:

*Table 3.1* Reflection questions about the proportion of learners with SEND

| Scenario | Reflection Questions |
|---|---|
| The overall proportion of children with SEND at the school is significantly higher than local and national averages | • Are there more learners with SEND at this school than other schools, or has the school been more effective at identifying needs? How do you know?<br>• What measures has the school put in place to ensure that the identification of SEND is accurate?<br>• Are there any moderation (or other) processes in place to improve the reliability of assessment of SEND and to ensure alignment with other local schools?<br>• How does the proportion of learners with SEND at the school vary over time (for example, three-year trend data), and how does this compare with local/ national data? |
| The overall proportion of children with SEND at the school is significantly lower than local and national averages | • Are there fewer learners with SEND at this school than other schools, or has the school been more effective at meeting needs? How do you know?<br>• How confident are teachers at identifying SEND, adapting their teaching and liaising with the SENCO where additional support may be required?<br>• What is the local reputation of the school in relation to inclusion and meeting the needs for learners with SEND? Are potential parents/carers confident the school can meet the needs of their child?<br>• Is the school's admissions process as inclusive as it could be? How does the school know that learners with SEND are not being excluded at the point of admission or beforehand? |
| The proportion of children at SEN Support at the school is significantly higher than local averages, but the proportion with EHC plans is significantly lower | • Are school leaders confident that the significantly higher proportion of learners at SEN Support is not due to a lack of high-quality inclusive teaching (quality-first teaching)?<br>• How many learners has the school supported to secure a needs assessment from the local authority? What proportion of these resulted in an EHC plan being issued?<br>• What is the school's SEN Support offer? Is it adequate in meeting the volume and complexity of needs?<br>• What training and CPD have teachers had over the past two years to support them in meeting the needs of learners with SEND? |

*Table 3.2* Analysis by primary areas of need – Lady Videtta High School

| | Proportion of Learners by Primary Area of Need (%) | | | | | | | | | | | | | |
| --- | --- | --- | --- | --- | --- | --- | --- | --- | --- | --- | --- | --- | --- | --- |
| | Specific Learning Difficulty | Moderate Learning Difficulty | Severe Learning Difficulty | Profound & Multiple Learning Difficulty | Social, Emotional and Mental Health | Speech, Language and Communications Needs | Hearing Impairment | Visual Impairment | Multi-Sensory Impairment | Physical Disability | Autistic Spectrum Disorder | Other Difficulty/Disability | SEN support but no specialist assessment of type of need | Total |
| **Lady Videtta High School** | 4.7 | 29.5 | 0.0 | 0.0 | 25.7 | 23.8 | 1.3 | 1.2 | 0.8 | 0.3 | 2.9 | 4.1 | 5.7 | 100 |
| **Blackpool** | 5.6 | 23.2 | 0.3 | 0.0 | 21.0 | 39.0 | 1.3 | 1.1 | 0.8 | 2.7 | 3.2 | 1.4 | 0.4 | 100 |
| **England** | 9.5 | 20.9 | 0.6 | 0.3 | 16.3 | 30.6 | 1.7 | 0.9 | 0.3 | 2.8 | 7.9 | 3.9 | 4.3 | 100 |

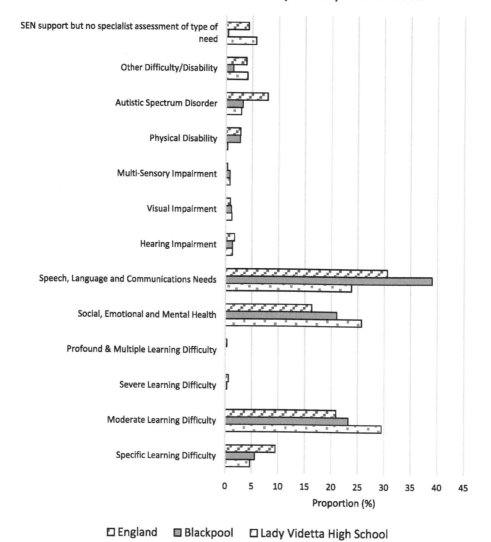

## Proportion of Learners with SEND by Primary Area of Need

☐ England   ▣ Blackpool   ☐ Lady Videtta High School

*Figure 3.1* Analysis by primary areas of need – Lady Videtta High School

1. The proportion of learners with Moderate Learning Difficulties, Other Difficulty/Disability or SEN Support with no specialist assessment of type of need is higher at Lady Videtta High School than it is locally. These three areas of need are similar in that they can sometimes be inappropriately used as broad 'catch-all' type categories. This suggests that accurate identification of needs may be an issue at Lady Videtta High School and should be explored further. That being said, two of these areas are in line with national data, so part of the issue may be to do with local approaches to identification rather than the school itself.

2. It is also notable that the proportion of learners with Speech, Language and Communication Needs is lower than both Blackpool and England. Could it be that some of those learners with a broader identification of SEND (for example, Moderate Learning Difficulties) actually have unidentified Speech, Language and Communication Needs? Do the processes for identifying these needs have an appropriate level of validity and reliability as well as specialist input?

3. The proportion of learners with Social, Emotional and Mental Health needs is higher at Lady Videtta High School than Blackpool and England. What provision does the school have in place to support wellbeing, and what does this data suggest about the effectiveness of this provision? Is the school confident that unidentified, and therefore unmet, needs are not becoming anxiety issues over time? Are there any particular groups of learners who are most at risk of developing Social, Emotional and Mental Health difficulties, and are the school's resources aligned to addressing this?

4. The proportion of learners with Autism Spectrum Disorder is in line with local data but significantly below national data. From a positive perspective, it may be that autism provision at the school and locally is highly effective, with many learners having their needs met and therefore not being recorded as having SEND on the census. However, school leaders will want to assure themselves that there is not a significant under-identification of autism needs. From a more challenging perspective, it may be that the families do not have confidence in local autism provision and services and are actively choosing to send their children to schools outside the area.

Occasionally, SENCOs have used the school-level underlying data to identify other schools with a similar context and profile of SEND to their own school. They have then made contact with their counterpart in the 'twinned school' to compare approaches and exchange ideas. This is an underused but potentially powerful use of this publicly available data.

## *Summary of Other Data Sources for SEND*

The same webpage that contains the annual data sets for SEND identification also has annual data sets related to EHC plans (DfE, 2023e). This includes a breakdown of the number of EHC plans issued during the year, the total number of EHC plans in place and the number and proportion of EHC plans issued within the statutory expectation of 20 weeks.

Buried further down on the same website is an underutilised but highly useful document that provides a summary of the many data sources related to SEND (DfE, 2023a). This document is updated regularly and contains links to around 30 relevant data sources that have a SEND-specific breakdown. The end of the document also has an overall analysis and summary of the data sources. Some of the data sources referenced include the following:

- Early years SEN prevalence
- Phonics screening check
- Attainment at key stages one, two and four
- Outcomes for looked-after children (LAC)
- Destination measures at key stages four and five
- Absence
- Progression into higher education
- Exclusions and suspensions
- SEND tribunals (including appeals)
- Employment and earnings
- Autism waiting times – National Health Service (NHS)
- Office for National Statistics (ONS) disability statistics

### Gov.UK Open Data Hub

Another data repository hidden within the government's website is the *Open Data Hub*, which contains a range of large machine-readable data sets published by central government, local authorities and public bodies (Gov UK, 2023). This data spans fourteen different categories: business and economy, crime and justice, defence, education, environment, government, government spending, health, mapping, society, towns and cities, transport, digital service performance and government reference data.

The Open Data Institute (ODI) defines open data as 'data that anyone can access, use and share' (ODI, 2016), so this can be used by schools if it adds value. Within the education section of the data hub, there are a small number of data sets that may of use in relation to SEND, such as data related to access arrangements for GCSE and A-level. However, the data sets available come with a 'health warning' as they are not always the most recent and they may require some cleansing to be used in a meaningful way.

### Provision Maps

SENCOs are increasingly using provision maps to record and monitor the range of different interventions in place for pupils with SEND. This can include impact data based on evaluations of interventions and the associated costs. Some SENCOs are using commercial, purpose-built software to map provision, whilst others are using less sophisticated solutions built with Microsoft Excel or Word. Irrespective of the methodology, provision maps can be used to help SENCOs to determine which interventions are most effective and which represent the best value for money.

Some of the SENCOs and school leaders interviewed for this book commented that their provision maps have been useful in supporting discussions about SEND funding with the local authority. More specifically, data from provision maps is being used to demonstrate where insufficient funding has been delegated by local authorities in relation to the SEN notional budget and/or high needs top-up funding.

### Apples and Pears

This chapter has focused on how a range of different data sources can be used to provide insights into pupils with special educational needs and the effectiveness of their provision. It has also suggested how data can be used for benchmarking, but great care should be taken when comparing pupils with SEND. Every pupil with SEND is an individual, so any comparisons of individuals or groups are unlikely to represent comparing like with like. It is not even like the idiom of comparing 'apples and pears' as this suggests there are two discrete groups. Extending the analogy further, it is helpful to think of this as more like comparing many different fruits from a basket of fruits rather than two types of fruit. This is not to say that benchmarking for pupils with SEND is wrong, but rather that it is useful to be aware of the limitations of the validity and reliability of such comparisons. Ultimately, the more nuanced any comparisons and insights are, the lower the risk that pupils with SEND are considered inappropriately as one homogenous group.

## Data Literacy for SENCOs

A consistent concern amongst the SENCOs interviewed is a lack of confidence in relation to using data. This is not limited to those who have been SENCOs for a long time since similar confidence issues arose from newer SENCOs, including those who are Gen Z. At the heart of the SENCOs' fears about data is the perception that they need to become highly proficient in data manipulation and analysis. In the words of one SENCO, 'I'm a teacher, not a data scientist.'

There is a widespread and fundamental misconception here, since the majority of SENCOs believe they need to have advanced data skills. Such skills may be useful, but they are not essential. To be effective in the role, SENCOs do not need to be data analysts, but they do need to be data literate. SENCOs need to be able to do basic data manipulation and analysis, and they need to understand the data well enough to be able to ask for anything else they need from those who are proficient in data analysis with more advanced skills.

When it comes to articulating what data literacy means in practice for SENCOs, Howieson et al. (2023, p. 148) suggest the following elements developed from Mandinach and Gummer (2016) are core:

- Understanding data sources
- Data collection and analysis
- Interpreting data
- Data-informed decision making
- Collaborating with stakeholders
- Data protection and privacy
- Continuous professional development

Whilst this is fine in principle and works at a strategic level, it can still feel nebulous to SENCOs, who are unsure where to start with the practical task of improving their data literacy. Therefore, it is suggested the following five steps shown in Figure 3.2 are a useful starting point for SENCOs in the early stages of their data literacy journey.

To help SENCOs understand the practicalities of these five steps, each is unpacked further later. Step two, the basics of Excel, is discussed last and in more detail as this includes some detailed step-by-step skills development.

## Data Familiarisation

Data familiarisation is about knowing what data sets you have access to as a SENCO and what kinds of information you can draw from the data. Cursory glances or dipping in and out of the data is unlikely to be sufficient to become familiar with it. It is suggested that SENCOs spend time 'playing with the data' to see what they uncover, rather than only looking at data with a specific purpose in mind.

This chapter has already given many examples of data sets that SENCOs have access to, but it is also possible to create your own data sets. For example, SENCOs have data from their evaluations of interventions. If there are stakeholder surveys (e.g., children, families, staff, volunteers), SENCOs can ask for some questions on SEND to be included. SENCOs can record the rates of attendance and participation of pupils with SEND (and their families) at school community events, such as school productions, sports day and the summer fayre. The number of complaints is often monitored in schools, but what about the number of compliments that SENCOs receive from families when provision is effective?

There is plenty of data out there. As a SENCO, immerse yourself in the richness of the data. This investment in time will pay dividends in the long run.

## Visuals for Communication

Using visuals for communication can be powerful, but this is rarely done well in society at large, let alone in schools where there are enormous time pressures and workload issues. Visuals such

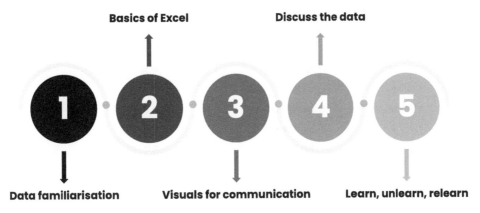

*Figure 3.2* Five steps towards data literacy

as graphs, charts and infographics can be used to communicate a specific point, but often they are used simply as an alternative way to access the data.

As an example, consider a data set containing the reading ages of a group of children before and after a term of literacy interventions. For ease, the interventions are provided to all children in the class, but the target group is children with communication and interaction needs. Table 3.3 shows some fictitious data of this sort that a SENCO may have collected.

The questions are how the SENCO evaluates the impact of the intervention and how this assessment is communicated to others. Data related to individual pupils can contribute to individual progress monitoring and sharing progress with families and with pupils themselves, but grouped data also has value. The SENCO might start by calculating the pre- and post-average reading ages for different groups of pupils. As shown in Table 3.4, this can be used to calculate the average increase in reading age per group. It can also show any additional increase beyond what might have been expected had pupils made the four months typical termly progress for all pupils had there been no intervention.

Now it comes to using visuals to communicate the data. Figure 3.3 shows a simple representation of the pre and post data in Table 3.4, but what is the key message the chart is attempting to communicate? Is it the heights of the bars in the chart that are important, or is it the respective gaps between the pre and post bars? Is the key feature the low reading age and low intervention impact for pupils with cognition and learning needs? Or is it something else? The point is that without further steering, different people will read different things into this visual representation of the data.

If it is the increase or relative increase (against no intervention) for each of the pupil groups, then Figure 3.4 is arguably an improved visualisation of the data.

*Table 3.3* Class reading ages pre- and post-literacy intervention

| Name | Gender | Broad Area of SEND | Reading Age (January) | Reading Age (April) |
|------|--------|--------------------|-----------------------|---------------------|
| Alex | F | No SEND | 8.4 | 8.7 |
| Bao | M | C&I | 7.5 | 8.3 |
| Cassie | F | No SEND | 8.9 | 9.1 |
| Dakota | F | No SEND | 9.5 | 9.8 |
| Ellen | F | SEMH | 8.7 | 9.1 |
| Frank | M | C&L | 6.6 | 6.8 |
| Gemma | F | C&I | 8.5 | 9.1 |
| Helen | F | C&L | 6.7 | 6.9 |
| Isaac | M | No SEND | 8.5 | 8.8 |
| Jordan | M | No SEND | 8.7 | 9.1 |
| Katie | F | No SEND | 8.3 | 8.5 |
| Lisa | F | No SEND | 7.9 | 8.2 |
| Mohammed | M | C&I | 8.1 | 8.9 |
| Noah | M | C&I | 7.9 | 8.5 |
| Ollie | M | No SEND | 10.4 | 10.6 |
| Polly | F | SEMH | 10.7 | 10.9 |
| Quinn | M | C&I | 8.4 | 8.8 |
| Riley | M | C&I | 7.7 | 8.4 |
| Saatvik | M | No SEND | 9.2 | 9.9 |
| Taylor | F | SEMH | 8.2 | 8.3 |
| Umar | M | No SEND | 9.1 | 9.6 |
| Vicky | F | No SEND | 8.3 | 8.5 |
| Will | M | No SEND | 8.4 | 9.2 |
| Xin | M | C&L | 5.9 | 5.9 |
| Yvonne | F | No SEND | 8.8 | 9.1 |
| Zara | F | SEMH | 8.5 | 8.7 |

*Table 3.4* Average increase in reading age for different pupil groups

|  | *Average Reading Age (January)* | *Average Reading Age (April)* | *Average Increase in Reading Age* | *Average Added Increase in Reading Age Beyond Typical Termly Progress (four months) for All Pupils* |
|---|---|---|---|---|
| All Pupils | 8.38 | 8.76 | 0.38 | 0.05 |
| Boys | 8.18 | 8.68 | 0.49 | 0.16 |
| Girls | 8.57 | 8.84 | 0.27 | -0.06 |
| SEND | 7.95 | 8.35 | 0.40 | 0.07 |
| No SEND | 8.80 | 9.16 | 0.36 | 0.03 |
| C&I | 8.02 | 8.67 | 0.65 | 0.32 |
| C&L | 6.40 | 6.53 | 0.13 | -0.20 |
| SEMH | 9.03 | 9.25 | 0.23 | -0.11 |

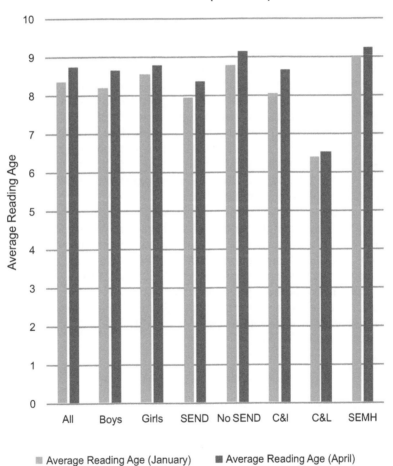

*Figure 3.3* Termly increase in average reading age for different pupil groups

The forms of visualisation in Figure 3.4 improve communication because it is now clearer that the intervention has had a significant impact on the target group of pupils (those with communication and interaction needs). This visualisation has also yielded some additional information, which is that there are three groups of pupils where the average increase in reading age is less than the average expected increase for all pupils had there been no intervention in place. This may warrant the SENCO looking further into understanding why this might be the case. In particular, the intervention appears to have had a positive impact on boys' reading ages, but

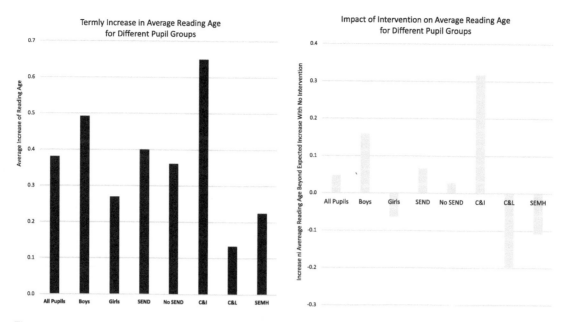

*Figure 3.4* Termly increase in average reading age and impact of intervention on average reading age for different pupil groups

not for girls'. Is there something about the nature or content of the intervention that could have caused this?

Returning to the original purpose of the intervention is often helpful. In this instance, the SENCO wanted to accelerate the increase in reading ages for pupils with communication and interaction needs. The literacy intervention was designed to do this. Figure 3.5 shows how the impact of the intervention might be communicated.

This is an example of highlighting particular aspects of the data to communicate specific points. It is of course important not to use such data visualisation and communication techniques to mislead people. Therefore, it is generally good practice to provide access to the wider data set and targeted visuals to support the specific points being communicated. When it comes to SENCOs considering how much of their precious time should be spent on creating such visuals, the advice from Pickles (2023) is only to spend time on graphs that will impact on pupil outcomes.

As an aside related to this example, there is an explicit claim here that the additional increase in reading ages is a direct consequence of the literacy intervention. It is of course very difficult in such circumstances to establish cause and effect as there are so many other variables involved. However, this does not mean such arguments should not be put forward. Ultimately, it is true that the literacy intervention did take place and that the reading ages for the target group did increase. So causal arguments can be made, but it is important to remain reflective and open-minded to alternative reasons for what has been observed.

## Discuss the Data

To support SENCOs in building up their confidence with data, it is important that they take opportunities to discuss how they have undertaken their analysis and any patterns they are finding. The more SENCOs talk about their data, the more feedback and alternative opinions they will encounter. This will help them to refine their interpretation skills and to think about new ways of communicating any key points.

One secondary school SENCO talked about how they have a 'SEND chart of the month' that they present to the leadership team. It can be on any aspect of SEND, but it essentially familiarises the wider leadership team with a more specialist subset of the data than they typically encounter. Figure 3.6 is an anonymised example of one such chart, which was based on a series of SEND learning walks. The SENCO observed that teachers were spending less direct time with pupils with SEND because teaching assistants were being deployed instead. The SENCO collated some data over the course of a couple of weeks and used it to produce a graph similar to Figure 3.6. This was raised this with the leadership team as the SENCO felt it was not right that the pupils with the most complex learning needs had the least time with the most qualified teaching professional in the room.

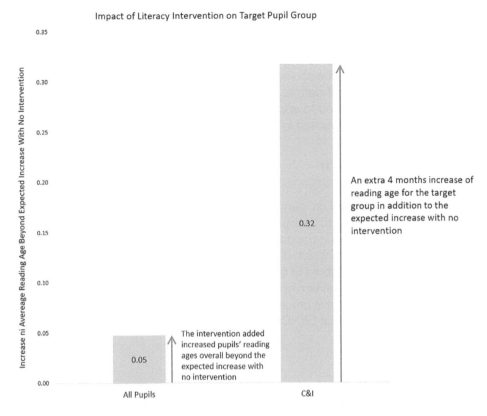

*Figure 3.5* Impact of literacy intervention on target group

Average direct teacher time received per pupil per lesson (seconds)

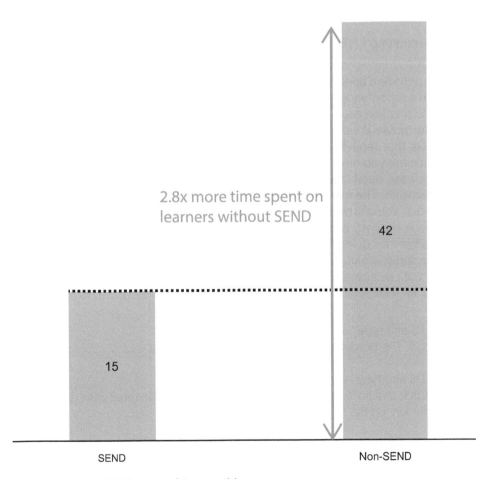

*Figure 3.6* Example of a 'SEND chart of the month'

This sort of deliberate and proactive discussion of SEND-related data is a good way for SENCOs to accelerate their data literacy. However, some SENCOs are afraid of making mistakes with data or misinterpreting it in a way that embarrasses them in front of their colleagues. When working with data, there needs to be an acceptance from all that mistakes will occur. This could be considered a blessing in disguise when it comes to developing data literacy, since the ability to identify anomalies in the data is a valuable skill. If mistakes are made, then this gives an opportunity to learn lessons and to apply them in the future. The principle of lessons learned becoming lessons applied is discussed in more detail in Chapter 4.

## *Learn, Unlearn and Relearn*

Much of this chapter has focused on learning to use different types of data and developing data literacy. However, it is important to recognise that schools and SENCOs do not exist in a vacuum. The world is constantly changing; data analytics and artificial intelligence (AI) are changing the way we work and the ways in which data and insights can be obtained and utilised.

For SENCOs, this means that some of the skills they learn may need to be unlearned at some point in the future, followed by relearning an alternative skill. The ability to learn, unlearn and relearn is a metacognitive skill that is crucial for the fast-paced and rapidly changing educational and technological environment that SENCOs are operating in.

## *Basics of Excel*

The purpose of this chapter is not to provide lessons in how to use Microsoft Excel, but when it comes to data literacy, there are five basic Excel skills that SENCOs feel are essential when it comes to data literacy:

- Using basic formulae
- Creating graphs
- Applying filters
- Sorting lists
- Conditional formatting

This chapter will provide a brief introduction to each of these Excel skills and signpost where you can access more support should that be helpful. Some exercises and instructions are provided to get started and practice each of the basic skills.

**Using basic formulae** is simple and can save you a lot of time and effort. Essentially, if there is a repetitive task that requires a calculator, Excel can almost certainly help you to be more efficient, which means you have more time to focus on the important business of children. For example, suppose ten pupils have completed a numeracy assessment, which is made up of three sub-assessments. The marks for each of the ten pupils are recorded on a spreadsheet, as shown in Figure 3.7. You will need to create this sheet to use with the following exercises.

The total score is needed, and this is found by adding together the scores of the three sub-assessments. Rather than doing this calculation by hand for each pupil and entering the numerical answers onto the spreadsheet, a formula can be used to automate the process. We will start with Lee. We want to put Lee's total score into cell F3, but instead of doing the specific calculation of 41 + 43 + 46, we will instead add together the three cells C3, D3 and E3. This is done as follows:

- Click on cell F3 and type '='.
- Click on cell C3. The border of the cell will start moving.
- Type '+'.
- Click on cell D3 and type '+'.
- Click on cell E3. It should look like Figure 3.8 as it's showing the three cells it will add together.
- Press the enter key on the keyboard.

Lee's total score of 130 should now appear in cell F3.

We would now like to repeat the equivalent calculation for the other nine students. This is where your hard work entering the addition formula earlier pays off. Click on cell F3 and a green

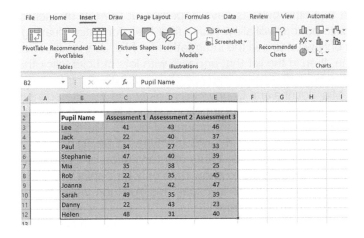

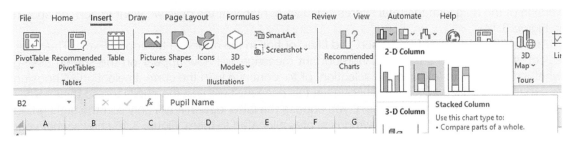

*Figure 3.11* Creating a stacked bar chart in Excel

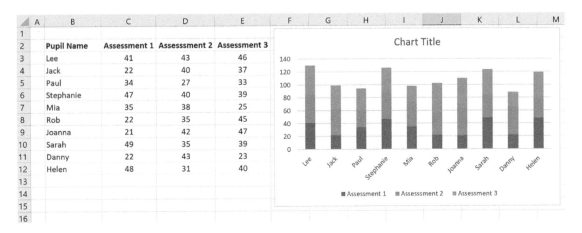

*Figure 3.12* Example of a stacked bar chart

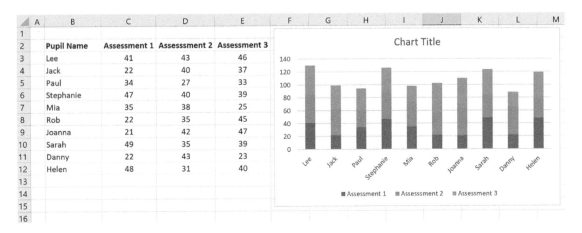

*Figure 3.13* Turning on filtering in Excel

You should notice that filter buttons have appeared at the top of each column in the table. Clicking on one of these buttons will allow you to filter the information, leaving only what you want to see. Suppose we only want to see the information for Mia, Joanna and Danny. Select the filter button for pupil name, then in the list that appears with lots of ticks, click the tick for 'select all', which will make all the ticks disappear. You can then tick only the information you want to see, which in our case is Mia, Joanna and Danny. Select okay and the filtered information appears.

In this example, we filtered to see information related to specific pupils. However, the real power of filtering is to see information for groups of pupils. More generally, SENCOs can use filters to only show the data for pupils with particular types of SEND or those who are in particular classes or year groups. You can filter by types of intervention or by age. Multiple filters can be applied at the same time, for example to show data only for pupils with SEMH in year nine.

For more information on using filters in Excel, this YouTube video is a good place to start: www.youtube.com/watch?v=BtiVbY7Ihqw.

**Sorting lists** is a useful feature of Excel. Returning to the numeracy assessments, we may wish to sort the data so it is in order from highest total score to lowest total score. Using the version of the data with the total scores calculated, highlight the cells we want to sort, as shown in Figure 3.14.

As we did earlier, look for the 'sort and filter' option in the ribbon at the top of Excel. This time, select 'sort largest to smallest'. An important message will now appear on the screen asking whether you want to 'expand the selection' or to 'continue with the current selection'. Choosing to expand the selection is the right option in this case as it will sort the pupils too so their names are still next to their correct scores. If you choose the latter option it will only sort the highlighted cells, and the pupils will have the wrongs scores allocated to them. Figure 3.15 shows what your list should look like if you have sorted and expanded correctly.

| | A | B | C | D | E | F | G |
|---|---|---|---|---|---|---|---|
| 1 | | | | | | | |
| 2 | | **Pupil Name** | Assessment 1 | Assesssment 2 | Assessment 3 | Total | |
| 3 | | Lee | 41 | 43 | 46 | 130 | |
| 4 | | Jack | 22 | 40 | 37 | 99 | |
| 5 | | Paul | 34 | 27 | 33 | 94 | |
| 6 | | Stephanie | 47 | 40 | 39 | 126 | |
| 7 | | Mia | 35 | 38 | 25 | 98 | |
| 8 | | Rob | 22 | 35 | 45 | 102 | |
| 9 | | Joanna | 21 | 42 | 47 | 110 | |
| 10 | | Sarah | 49 | 35 | 39 | 123 | |
| 11 | | Danny | 22 | 43 | 23 | 88 | |
| 12 | | Helen | 48 | 31 | 40 | 119 | |
| 13 | | | | | | | |
| 14 | | | | | | | |

Figure 3.14 Highlighting cells in Excel ready for sorting

| | A | B | C | D | E | F | G |
|---|---|---|---|---|---|---|---|
| 1 | | | | | | | |
| 2 | | **Pupil Name** | Assessment 1 | Assesssment 2 | Assessment 3 | Total | |
| 3 | | Lee | 41 | 43 | 46 | 130 | |
| 4 | | Stephanie | 47 | 40 | 39 | 126 | |
| 5 | | Sarah | 49 | 35 | 39 | 123 | |
| 6 | | Helen | 48 | 31 | 40 | 119 | |
| 7 | | Joanna | 21 | 42 | 47 | 110 | |
| 8 | | Rob | 22 | 35 | 45 | 102 | |
| 9 | | Jack | 22 | 40 | 37 | 99 | |
| 10 | | Mia | 35 | 38 | 25 | 98 | |
| 11 | | Paul | 34 | 27 | 33 | 94 | |
| 12 | | Danny | 22 | 43 | 23 | 88 | |
| 13 | | | | | | | |

Figure 3.15 Example of a sorted list in Excel

For more information on sorting data in Excel, this YouTube video is a good place to start: www.youtube.com/watch?v=Bm_uWOUiUFI.

**Conditional formatting** is the final basic Excel skill that SENCOs felt was essential. Conditional formatting is a way of automatically highlighting cells if they meet particular criteria. Returning to the numeracy assessment data set one final time, let us suppose that scores under 30 for each of the individual assessments are a cause for concern and that scores over 45 are a cause for celebration. With a small data set, we can clearly just look for scores that meet these criteria, but for larger data sets, this would be very time consuming. This is where conditional formatting can save a lot of time.

Start by highlighting the thee columns of data, then navigate to 'conditional formatting', 'highlight cells rules' and 'less than . . .', as shown in Figure 3.16.

We want to highlight in red any scores less than 30 as they are a cause for concern, so enter 30 into the box. Repeat these steps, but this time select 'greater than . . .' and use the number 45 and 'green fill'. Figure 3.17 shows what should be entered in both boxes.

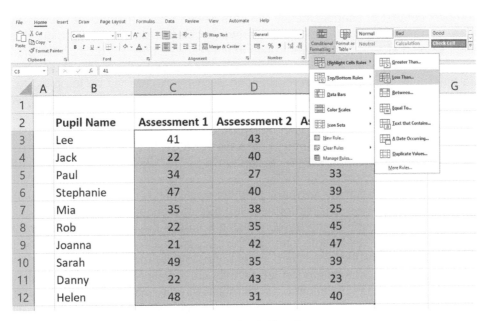

*Figure 3.16* Getting started with conditional formatting in Excel

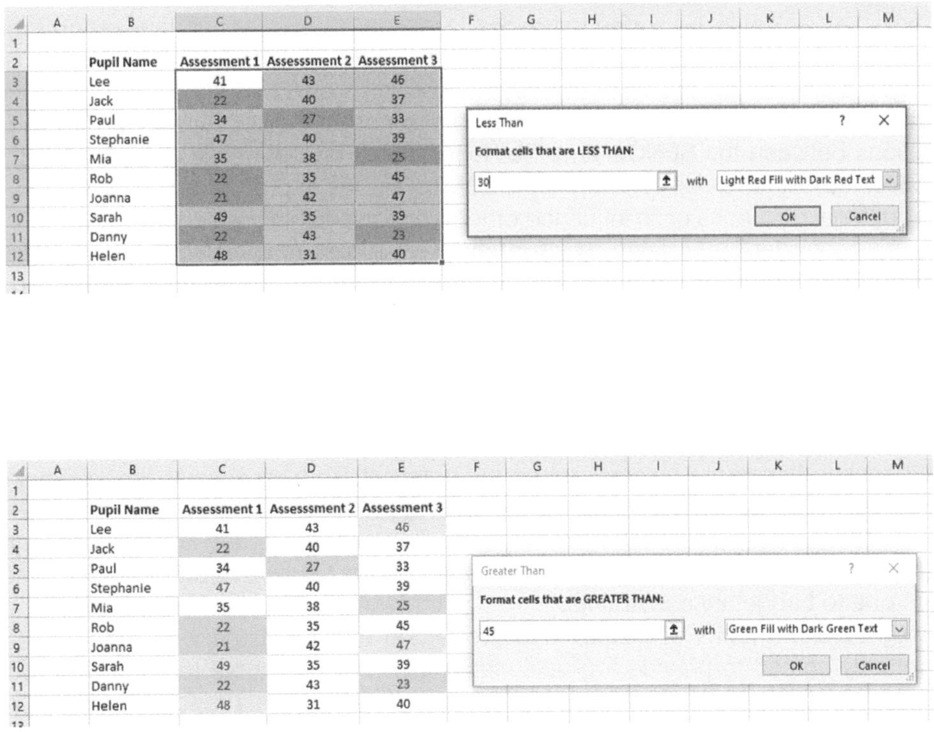

*Figure 3.17* Conditional formatting boxes in Excel

The table will now automatically highlight scores lower than 30 in red and scores higher than 45 in green. This form of visualisation is powerful in its own right. It helps SENCOs to see visually whether many pupils are struggling with a particular assessment or whether individual pupils are struggling across multiple assessments.

For more information on conditional formatting in Excel, this YouTube video is a good place to start: www.youtube.com/watch?v=Jp29JYGq5Hw.

## Other Data Concepts

There are three other concepts when working with data that SENCOs may find helpful: single source of the truth, reporting by exception and watermelon reporting. Each will now be covered in turn, starting with the importance of having a single source of the truth.

The complex context of schools means they are likely to have many overlapping data sets. Sometimes, equivalent data will not match between different data sets, perhaps due to the data being gathered at a slightly different point in time or via a different data collection method. Therefore, care should be taken to determine which data becomes the single source of the truth to ensure that future comparisons are comparing like with like. It may be tempting to choose data that is the closest fit for the story you want to tell, but the value of consistency will bring greater rewards over time.

Reporting by exception is an approach more commonly associated with the corporate world than schools, but there is an argument it could save SENCOs time and allow them to prioritise their efforts. The principle of reporting by exception is to only report and escalate matters that fall outside of a pre-agreed set of parameters.

From a SEND perspective, there are many potential applications of reporting by exception. For example, every SENCO is responsible for ensuring that appropriate SEND provision is in place and is effective for each pupil on the SEND register. Suppose the Headteacher is the SENCO's line manager. How should the Headteacher get the necessary assurance that provision is working as it should be? At one extreme, there is the hands-off approach, which is based on completely trusting the SENCO to do a good job as they are a senior leader within the school and will raise any issues or areas of concern. At the other extreme, there is the micro-management approach, which is based on the SENCO providing a regular update of provision for all pupils. Reporting by exception seeks to find a structured and pragmatic third way that falls between the two approaches described earlier.

The pre-agreed criteria might be that if a pupil's SEND provision is not in place and agreed with parents within a week of being added to the SEND register, then an exceptions report is provided for the Headteacher. Similarly, the pre-agreed criteria might state that if the academic progress of pupils with SEND falls below 85% of expectations, then an exceptions report is provided for the Headteacher. This process effectively escalates issues as they occur and facilitates targeted conversations between the SENCO and the Headteacher on the pupils where SEND provision is ineffective. It provides an opportunity for the Headteacher to provide advice and guidance, to release additional resources or to influence other functions within the school.

Lastly, let us consider RAG ratings, which is when red, amber and green colours are used to indicate through data reporting where things are either on track (green), not on track (red) or somewhere in between (amber). This is not dissimilar to the use of conditional formatting described earlier in the chapter. Occasionally, BRAG rating is used, where blue indicates significant over-achievement. Watermelon reporting is a reference to RAG status that reports everything is on track, but the reality is that it is not. Like a watermelon, it is green on the outside but red on the inside.

An obvious initial question is why any professional working in a school would provide a RAG report suggesting things are on track when they are not. To help answer this question, let us consider a situation raised by a Headteacher during one of the interviews for this book. The Headteacher explained that in their school they had an above average number of children with EHC plans who needed 1:1 support, but they also had a below average number of teaching assistants due to budgetary constraints.

Following several months of difficult and protracted conversations with the local authority, they reluctantly agreed to provide top-up funding to allow the school to employ an additional teaching assistant. However, they were clear that if this additional resource did not result in SEND provision being effective for this particular child, then the resource would not be continued for the following year.

When it came to the review point, the Headteacher was asked to provide an update on the impact of the additional resource. The reality was that the child had complex needs, and even with the additional support, progress was slow and hard. However, the Headteacher was also acutely aware that it would be a far worse situation without the teaching assistant. The family was happy with the support in place, and from the Headteacher's perspective it freed up resources for the many other pupils with SEND.

In this situation, the Headteacher confessed that they did not want 'to bite the hand that feeds [them]'. Therefore, he provided a green RAG status update as part of his report, which resulted in the school being allowed to keep the teaching assistant, despite the fact that the local authority would have likely assessed the situation with a red RAG status. The Headteacher effectively used watermelon reporting. Despite the clear ethical implications of this decision, the Headteacher was adamant that the ends justified the means in this instance.

Watermelon reporting is just one form of strategic misrepresentation (Silva and Portman, 2019) – or, as some people call it, 'lying' (Vincent, 2022). When strategic misrepresentation occurs, it should not be assumed it is for personal gain as the ethics are often complex and commonly due to optimism bias rather than deliberate deception. However, this issue can occur at multiple levels in different ways, so it is useful to be aware of it and to take steps to encourage transparency. In practice this will require psychological safety to make teams more effective (McWilliam and Toner, 2021), alongside an assurance that any emerging issues are responded to constructively and proportionately rather than punitively.

## Artificial Intelligence in Schools

Although artificial intelligence (AI) has been around for decades (Farina and Lavazza, 2023), it has arguably become mainstreamed in society since the launch of Chat GPT (Ipsos, 2023). It is now difficult to discuss data without considering AI, which is why it is included as a section within this chapter. There remains significant debate about the affordances and constraints of AI (Farina and Lavazza, 2023), but recent developments provide clear evidence that we have moved from an AI winter into an AI summer (Entefly, 2023).

One of the criticisms often levelled at generative AI is the fact that it is capable of creating absurd content that appears credible (Thorp, 2023). Content of this type is more generally referred to as an 'AI hallucination', and it is often characterised as being something that humans would immediately recognise as being ridiculous because it is inaccurate, prejudiced or unsuitable (Malvania and Majumdar, 2023).

A good example to illustrate AI hallucination is the early generative AI used to create facial images. In order to artificially generate images of faces, the AI was drawing on a bank of hundreds of thousands (likely millions) of existing images of real faces. Many of these images were available in the public domain, and there were a significant number that showed individuals in front of a horizon. Consequentially, the AI incorrectly identified the horizon as one of the features of a face. When asked to generate a face, it would often include a horizontal line passing through the neck. A human would have realised immediately that this was wrong, but the AI did not as this was an AI hallucination. In this simple example, the AI hallucination was easy to identify and address. However, such hallucinations are more difficult to recognise as contexts become more complex. In practice, those using AI need to ensure they build in anti-hallucinogenic workflows to reduce the likelihood of such peculiar outputs.

Let us consider an educational use of AI that is being used in a primary school. The AI is being used to assess pupils' work and then to provide formative feedback for individual pupils. There was initially some concern from teachers that the AI-generated formative assessment would be too generic, and there was scepticism from others that the approach would be less impactful than using their own professional expertise. Therefore, the teachers spent many hours checking each set of feedback before sharing it with the children. They found that they were impressed with what the AI had produced and therefore decided to continue using it. Moving forwards, it was decided not to spend hours checking what the generative AI was producing and instead for teachers to use the gained time to work directly with children.

This example showcases the transformational impact that AI can have from an educational perspective, but it also shows how quickly professionals can become reliant on this emerging technology. If an AI hallucination arises within pupils' feedback in the future, will this be picked up by the teacher? Do the benefits of this approach outweigh the risks of receiving inaccurate or unsuitable feedback? Increasingly, it will become necessary for users of AI to embed anti-hallucinogenic workflows into their processes to minimise the chances of such issues occurring.

One of the concerns often cited about the use of generative AI, and indeed digital technologies more broadly, is that that it can amplify the inherent biases that exist within society, such as misogyny (Heikkila, 2022; Roberts and Marchais, 2018). This raises an important ethical question about its use in a school context. Such risks also need to be counter-balanced by the reality that young people will be using AI technology irrespective of whether or not schools decide to use it. Therefore, there is arguably an inherent obligation on schools to help young people to understand the issues and opportunities of such technology.

During the interviews, all SENCOs were aware of AI, but very few had used it directly as part of their role. This is not generally due to ethical concerns such as those raised earlier, but because they are not sure how AI could be used in relation to SEND and because the opportunity has not naturally arisen.

The small number of SENCOs who are using AI had an optimistic perspective of its impact in relation to SEND. One SENCO shared how they had used generative AI to analyse their provision map and to make suggestions for how the planned interventions could be made more effective. The SENCO described this as being equivalent to the outcome from a SENCO brainstorming session at a conference, but instead of taking 30 minutes, it took 30 seconds.

---

### Box 3.1  Using ChatGPT to write a SEND strategy

The following prompt was used with ChatGPT to see what would happen when it was asked to generate a SEND strategy. It produced the following outcome in a few seconds.

**Prompt:**  Write a 500-word strategy for inclusion, special educational needs and disability for my primary school.

**Response:**  *Building an Inclusive Environment: A Strategy for Inclusion, Special Educational Needs, and Disability in [Primary School Name]*

### Introduction

Inclusion is not just a concept; it is a fundamental ethos that should permeate every aspect of our educational institution. At [Primary School Name], we believe in creating a supportive and enriching environment where every child feels valued, respected, and able to thrive. In this strategy, we outline our commitment to inclusion, addressing the needs of students with special educational needs and disabilities (SEND) to ensure they receive the support and opportunities they deserve.

### Creating an Inclusive Culture

Staff Training: Provide regular training sessions for all staff members to enhance their understanding of inclusion, SEND, and diverse learning needs. This training should focus on fostering empathy, understanding individual differences, and implementing inclusive teaching practices.

Promoting Respect and Acceptance: Encourage an atmosphere of respect, acceptance, and celebration of diversity among students, staff, and parents. Organise awareness campaigns, assemblies, and workshops to promote inclusivity and discourage discrimination or bullying.

Student Involvement: Involve students in creating an inclusive school culture by establishing peer support programs, student-led initiatives, and inclusive activities that encourage collaboration and empathy.

### Personalised Learning and Support

Individual Education Plans (IEPs): Develop personalised IEPs for students with SEND in collaboration with teachers, parents, and external support services. Ensure that these plans are regularly reviewed and adjusted to meet the evolving needs of each student.

Differentiated Instruction: Implement teaching strategies that cater to diverse learning styles and abilities within the classroom. Provide additional support, accommodations, or adaptations as necessary to enable all students to access the curriculum and participate fully.

Access to Resources: Ensure that students with SEND have access to appropriate resources, assistive technologies, and learning materials that support their individual needs and facilitate their learning journey.

## Collaboration and Partnership

Multi-Disciplinary Team Approach: Foster collaboration among teachers, teaching assistants, SENCOs (Special Educational Needs Coordinators), therapists, and external agencies to provide holistic support for students with SEND. Regular communication and coordination are essential to ensure a cohesive approach to meeting the diverse needs of students.

Engaging Parents and Carers: Establish open and transparent communication channels with parents and carers, involving them in the decision-making process regarding their child's education and support needs. Provide information, guidance, and opportunities for parents to actively participate in their child's learning journey.

## Community Engagement

Forge partnerships with local organisations, support groups, and agencies that specialise in SEND to access additional resources, expertise, and opportunities for our students. Collaborate with these stakeholders to organise workshops, events, and activities that benefit the wider community.

## Continuous Evaluation and Improvement

Data-Informed Decision-Making: Utilise data and feedback from various sources, including assessments, progress reports, and stakeholder surveys, to monitor the effectiveness of our inclusion strategy and identify areas for improvement.

Regular Review and Reflection: Conduct regular reviews of policies, practices, and interventions related to inclusion and SEND to ensure they align with best practices, legislative requirements, and the evolving needs of our school community.

Continuous Professional Development: Provide ongoing professional development opportunities for staff to enhance their knowledge, skills, and confidence in supporting students with SEND and promoting inclusion effectively.

## Conclusion

Inclusion is a journey, not a destination, and at [Primary School Name], we are committed to continually striving towards creating a truly inclusive environment where every child feels valued, supported, and empowered to reach their full potential. By implementing the strategies outlined in this document and fostering a culture of collaboration, respect, and continuous improvement, we aim to create a school where diversity is celebrated, and every student thrives.

## Reflection Questions

1. What is your assessment of the quality of the AI-generated SEND strategy? Would this be a useful starting point if you had to write a SEND strategy from scratch in your school?
2. Are there other strategic outputs where AI could be used to provide some of the required input?

Another SENCO explained that their perception of AI is as a form of assistive technology that can be used as a tool in the classroom. This could be asking the AI for help as an alternative to asking the teacher for help when a pupil gets stuck. In one school, they are using AI live in the classroom to adapt learning materials to make them more accessible for children with different reading ages. There are understandable concerns that use of generative AI by students to produce essays or homework in an educational context 'threatens to erode academic integrity' (Koplin and Hatherley, 2022). This raises important questions about the trade-off between academic integrity and improved accessibility.

From an efficiency perspective, a small number of SENCOs raised concerns about what AI might mean for the future of their job. Given that many aspects of the SENCO role are process driven, there is concern that AI could potentially be a more cost-effective alternative to having a SENCO at all. Although AI can help to automate repetitive tasks, it should be highlighted that AI is replacing tasks, not roles (McKendrick, 2018). The SENCO role is about both people and processes, so if the processes can be better handled by AI, it will become even more important to have SENCOs who have a deep understanding of SEND and have mature emotional intelligence. Being a fantastically organised administrator will cease to have the prominence that it does currently within the SENCO role.

Given that the use of AI in schools is still a relatively new phenomenon, it is worth sharing a few further points that will help to make the most of this rapidly growing technology. Firstly, there are often concerns about the quality and accuracy of the outputs produced by generative AI. Therefore, it is becoming increasingly common to use what is known as 'discriminative AI', which limits the data sources used by the technology. For example, the CEO of one Trust explained how their schools use their teacher-created curriculum resources as an LLM (Large Language Model).

Secondly, the schools that are ahead of the curve in their use of AI have been teaching their pupils how to be more effective with prompt engineering. For those for whom 'prompt engineering' is a new term, this is about improving the quality of the prompts put into AI. The fundamental principle is that more specific prompts are more likely to produce the required outputs: quality in, quality out.

Thirdly, it is important to think of AI as a tool rather than as a complete replacement for human thought and judgement. Much like the satellite navigation system in a car or even self-driving cars, humans need to be ready to intervene when the technology produces an AI hallucination.

## *ChatGPT's Top Ten for Inclusive Schools*

As part of the research into the use of AI to support schools in developing a more inclusive culture, ChatGPT was asked to create a list of ten strategies that SENCOs could use. This was the result:

Creating a more inclusive culture in your school requires intentional effort and a variety of strategies. Here are ten approaches you can consider:

1.  **Promote Diversity:** Celebrate the diversity within your school community by organising events, guest speakers, or cultural showcases that highlight different backgrounds, traditions, and perspectives.
2.  **Establish Inclusive Policies:** Review and update school policies to ensure they are inclusive and equitable for all students, staff, and families. This may include anti-discrimination policies, language access policies, and guidelines for accommodating diverse needs.
3.  **Train Staff:** Provide professional development workshops and training sessions for teachers and staff to increase their cultural competency, sensitivity, and awareness of diversity issues. This training should focus on fostering empathy, understanding, and inclusive teaching practices.
4.  **Create Safe Spaces:** Designate physical spaces within the school where students from marginalised groups feel safe and supported. These spaces can serve as resource centres, affinity groups, or multicultural clubs where students can connect with peers who share similar experiences.
5.  **Foster Inclusive Language:** Encourage the use of inclusive language and communication practices that respect gender identity, cultural differences, and diverse perspectives. This includes using gender-neutral pronouns, avoiding stereotypes, and promoting respectful dialogue.
6.  **Provide Accessibility:** Ensure that the school environment is accessible to students with disabilities by removing physical barriers, providing assistive technologies, and offering support services such as sign language interpreters or captioning for events.

7. **Engage Families and Communities:** Actively involve families and community members from diverse backgrounds in school decision-making processes, volunteer opportunities, and cultural events. Build partnerships with local organisations and businesses to support inclusive initiatives.

8. **Curriculum Diversity:** Incorporate diverse perspectives, histories, and voices into the curriculum across all subjects. Use inclusive teaching materials, literature, and educational resources that reflect the experiences of diverse populations and challenge stereotypes.

9. **Address Bias and Bullying:** Implement programmes and initiatives to address bias-based bullying, harassment, and discrimination. Provide training for students on bystander intervention, conflict resolution, and promoting respect for others.

10. **Evaluate and Adjust:** Regularly assess the effectiveness of your school's efforts to promote inclusivity through surveys, focus groups, and feedback mechanisms. Use data to identify areas for improvement and adjust strategies accordingly.

By implementing these strategies consistently and involving the entire school community, you can create a more inclusive culture where all students feel valued, respected, and supported to thrive academically and personally.

## Conclusion

This chapter has explored data for delivery in a myriad of theoretical and practical ways. It has shared the ways in which SENCOs are currently using data to help them in their role, but it has also made suggestions in the form of new ideas that SENCOs should consider trying. A key message from this chapter is for SENCOs to ensure that they have an appropriate level of data literacy, including the some of the basics of using Excel. Other data concepts such as reporting by exception and strategic misrepresentation have been discussed to help SENCOs further mature their confidence in using data for delivery. Lastly, the growing use of AI in schools was discussed, with the overarching message that SENCOs should give it a try to see what it can do to support them. It is important to be mindful about the ethics of AI and whether it might become sentient and act against humans, as these are valid concerns. However, these are the concerns of tomorrow, not today. In the words of mathematician Hannah Fry (paraphrased from machine-learning expert Andrew Ng), 'worrying about evil AI is a bit like worrying about overcrowding on Mars' (Fry, 2018, p. 14).

## Reflection Questions

1. Does your school have a policy on using AI to support teaching and learning? Has any serious consideration been given to using AI as an assistive technology to improve accessibility and to support adaptive teaching?

2. As a SENCO, what data sets do you routinely use in your role? What other data sets do you have access to, and why are they not used?

## Suggested Resources

1. *ChatGPT* is a freely available generative AI tool. It can write strategy, review documents and assess pupils' work. This type of AI could support you in both the educational and administrative aspects of your SENCO role. Don't knock it until you've tried it!
https://chat.openai.com/

2. The *Assistive Technology Mini-guide* is a freely-available resource commissioned and published by nasen (National Association for Special Educational Needs). It aims to provide practical strategies, insights and real-life examples of how assistive technology can revolutionise support for learning.
https://nasen.org.uk/atminiguide

# 4 Lessons Learned, Lessons Applied

Chapter 4 draws heavily on the interviews and conversations with SENCOs and senior leaders. The individual stories of the past that helped individual SENCOs to master their craft will be unpacked with their reflections on how they are applying that learning today. In particular, this chapter will reveal the advice that experienced SENCOs would have given to their younger selves earlier in their careers.

A theme of this chapter will be the notion of 'failing up' and how SENCOs use challenging professional situations as learning experiences to further develop their expertise in the role. Other themes to be discussed in this chapter include the way in which SENCOs manage the emotional toll of the role, how they remain resilient in the face of adversity and how they maintain an appropriate work-life balance.

SENCOs often need to maintain effective relationships within an adversarial context, where there are typically insufficient resources and funding available to meet the level of need. Chapter 4 will provide insights into the wisdom that SENCOs have developed on how to nurture and optimise key relationships in such circumstances. This includes their relationships with families, pupils with SEND, colleagues, school leaders and professionals from external services.

The chapter will conclude by considering the lessons that SENCOS have learnt through preparing for, and being part of, Ofsted inspections. From routine monitoring to the evidence they use to demonstrate their effectiveness during an Ofsted inspection, this chapter shines a light on the practical steps taken by SENCOs.

Peppered throughout the chapter are vignettes that provide insights to some of the situations that SENCOs have responded to as part of their role. Each vignette has a couple of reflection questions designed to help new SENCOs benefit from the experiences of their colleagues in the wider profession.

## The Benefit of Hindsight

One of the key themes in the discussions with SENCOs was the advice they would give to their younger self now that they have the benefit of hindsight. Such advice is likely to be useful for all SENCOs, but particularly for those who are at an early stage in their SENCO career.

### Getting Stuck and Trying Things

A reoccurring theme from SENCOs was deciding what to do when you do not know what to do. This situation seemed to come up frequently because of the individualised nature of each pupil with SEND. It seems that even when you think you have seen everything, something new comes up and it is hard to know what to do. The advice from one SENCO was to 'be brave and try something'. Another echoed the point about trying something, adding that if that does not work, keep trying until you find something that does work. Several SENCOs commented on the fact they had sometimes not put a particular intervention in place because they were not sure it was exactly right but that they later regretted this and ended up doing it anyway. In the words of one SENCO,

> When it comes to interventions, I learnt not to make perfect the enemy of good.

On the theme of trying, lots of SENCOs talked about the importance of figuring out 'the one thing that gives you a way in' for each child. They claim that every child has something that 'makes them tick' and that if you can 'find the hook and keep pulling it', you will have a breakthrough.

DOI: 10.4324/9781032634807-4

The notion of labels came up in these discussions as being a useful starting point to find out what works for children with SEND, but they also cautioned that an over-reliance on labels would inadvertently limit the scope for thinking creatively. As one SENCO put it, 'Labels can be helpful, but at the end of the day, it's not really about labels, it's about children. All children have spiky profiles. It's just about how spiky they are.'

There was a recognition from SENCOs that whilst their aspiration might be focused on doing the best for everybody all of the time, it was not always possible. Sometimes, SENCOs have to contend with budget constraints, waiting lists and staff capacity, so in the words of one SENCO, 'Accept that you can't do everything. Relax into the role. Control the things you can control and don't worry too much about the rest.'

## Career Development

Around 15% of the interviewed SENCOs had spent part of their career working in special schools or other specialist settings. Perhaps unsurprisingly, they were unanimous in their view that all SENCOs should spend some time in a specialist setting. They were clear this should be a substantive experience of at least a year rather than the occasional visit. When probed about the benefits of such exposure, many of the responses focused on the value of being able to monitor, recognise and celebrate small steps of progress as these are often giant leaps for the individual children concerned.

Other SENCOs talked about the importance of professional development throughout their career, but they emphasised that this should go beyond the 'routine CPD' provided by schools or local authorities. Some of the SENCOs had undertaken Masters studies and commented that this had opened up job opportunities for them as it gave them the edge over other candidates. They also argued that the academic rigour of such programmes helped them to develop and hone their critical thinking skills, which was useful in the day-to-day delivery of the SENCO role.

Several SENCOs had developed expertise in relation to a specific aspect of SEND by taking multiple qualifications in that area, by attending relevant conferences and by immersing themselves in relevant thought leadership. This most often focused on learning more about a type of SEND, such as dyslexia or ADHD, but occasionally it focused on an element of the processes related to SEND, such as screening, the deployment of teaching assistants or being part of local needs assessment panels. In any case, the notion of a SENCO having a specialism in addition to their broad expertise was generally considered to be a benefit.

There were some flippant comments made by SENCOs related to professional development, which had at least a semblance of substance to them. A few commented about the value of developing their skills in touch typing or professional writing given the volume of paperwork involved with the role. Another SENCO suggested a public speaking class or networking skills would be helpful. Perhaps the most tongue-in-cheek comment was made by the SENCO who suggested self-defence classes would be beneficial.

A few SENCOs made the point about the role being career-limiting. They were clear to emphasise that they thought the role should be career-enhancing because of its breadth and complexity, but this did not happen in practice because it was not as valued as other roles on the pathway to Headship. In primary schools, SENCOs felt that the literacy lead, numeracy lead or Designated Safeguarding Lead (DSL) roles were (unfairly) seen as being more relevant to Headship. In secondary schools, SENCOs felt that those seeking Headship were expected to follow a pastoral route or a teaching and learning route, whilst the SENCO role was perceived as being 'the worst of all worlds, rather than the best of both'.

When pressed on the answer to this problem, SENCOs were clear that it was not to avoid taking on the SENCO role but, once there, to advocate for it to have an equivalent status to other roles on the pathway to Headship. For example, several SENCOs noted that scheduled SEND plans are often the first to be cancelled when there is a capacity issue in school. This should not routinely be what happens, but it is sadly true in too many schools.

## Getting Practical and Tactical

The SENCOs had plenty of practical and tactical advice to share, but there were some points that came up over and over again. To begin with, it is important to be organised. The role has a lot of administration and paperwork requirements, so it is essential to keep on top of this to avoid becoming overwhelmed. Coupled with this is the need to prioritise. The simple reality is that there will always be something more you can do, but that does not mean you should do it. One SENCO stated,

> The expectations are infinite, but your time is finite. Learn to prioritise the things that will make the most impact. If you try to do everything, you will be burnt out very quickly.

Alongside administration, the need for good diary management was identified as being vital to the role. A few SENCOs described how they sometimes have moments of panic when they worry they have not invited everybody along to a meeting who needs to be there or if they have forgotten to contact a parent about something. Some of the SENCOs were fortunate enough to have administrative support, which they said was helpful, but only if managed effectively.

> Getting really good admin support is worth its weight in gold!

Several SENCOs advocated for getting other staff members involved with the process of identifying SEND and putting the appropriate provision in place. Many SENCOs described the isolation of the role and described the challenge of trying to get things done as one individual. One SENCO talked about the fact that she had no idea about the school's financial position as she was not part of the leadership team. As a result, requests for additional provision and resource kept getting blocked. This SENCO described her journey from being the person sitting in an office 'owning all thing SEND' to something that is now co-owned by teachers and leaders. The SENCO went on to describe how she 'hammered it home to senior leadership team so they are now much more clued up' on what is needed to get it right for pupils with SEND. Linking in with the behaviour lead was also identified as being important since behaviour is often about needs in any case.

Another recurring point was that SENCOs should not be afraid to ask for help when they need it. The issues are complex, and asking for help is not a sign of weakness or failure. As an example, one SENCO described a situation with a parent who continually went to tribunal over their dissatisfaction with the provision in place at the school. There was an EHC plan in place, but the parent had very specific views about how provision should be implemented without understanding the practicalities. The SENCO explained how she was expected to go to the tribunal meetings to be the representative for the school, but this was not something she had ever done before. At this point in her career, she was not sure whether she should ask for help or not. Reflecting on it now, she wishes she had, as what was actually lacking was direct support from the senior leadership team.

---

**Box 4.1 Sharing the administrative burden – getting others involved in SEND processes**

From a secondary school SENCO:

> When I joined my school, everything was in paper folders. Every referral, every pupil profile, every bit of paper there was for anything to do with SEND. There were rows upon rows of dusty old folders that no one ever went near. Worse still, all of these folders were in the SENCO's office. Most staff had no idea the folders were there, what was in them, or what they were for. Most staff weren't involved in the process of how those things came about. So why would they ever think to look at them, let alone to use them?
>
> The former SENCO would create the paperwork for individual children. She would give the child their targets, hand them to the teacher and that was it. The teaching staff were never involved in the process, so therefore they did not understand the process. As a result, there were frequent incidents of staff placing demands on the SENCO every time they wanted some extra provision in place because they did not understand the purpose of the provision that was already in place.
>
> So, my one piece of advice to all SENCOs is to streamline your paperwork and processes. Keep what is necessary and keep what is up to date, but if it is not adding any value, lose it quickly. Make your paperwork readily available to staff as it is they who can act on the information in the classroom. Get staff involved in the whole process from the outset. Show them the reports and keep them updated with what is going on. Get them to help with relevant aspects of the paperwork.

## Reflection Questions

1. What are the benefits and the dis-benefits of involving classroom and subject teachers with SEND administration?
2. In an increasingly digital world, is there any argument for using a paper-based approach to SEND administration?

There were many comments about the deployment of teaching assistants, such as how to achieve the right balance between supporting in classrooms and delivering targeted interventions, but no one approach came out as being dominant. If anything, the discussions emphasised the importance of contextual information in making decisions about the deployment of teaching assistants.

One thing that the SENCOs did largely agree on in relation to teaching assistants was that it is helpful if they develop some specialist expertise. For example, one SENCO reported that one of their teaching assistants had specialised in speech and language interventions and that another had specialised in trauma-informed approaches. The SENCO felt that having this sort of more specialist expertise on the team helped them to be more strategic in the role.

When it comes to recruiting teaching assistants, SENCOs had some sage words of advice. There was broad agreement that employing good teaching assistants is about more than choosing somebody just because they are a nice and kind person; it is also about identifying those with the right values who can become effective in the role.

Extending the theme of kindness, one SENCO explained how they thought that being kind was not always the right thing to do. When this was explored further, it turned out to be less about kindness and more about having clear boundaries and managing expectations. The SENCO was concerned that others sometimes took advantage of their kind nature and that this created additional workload pressures trying to achieve the unachievable because she did not want to let anybody down.

Another tactic shared by SENCOs was to buy in external specialist expertise and services rather than trying to create something in-house, which is typically less effective, more time consuming and more expensive in the long run. Such expertise included schools hiring their own speech and language therapists and educational psychologists directly rather than being solely dependent on local authority services. For services, many SENCOs recommended buying purpose-built provision mapping software and commercial screening tools to support monitoring and early identification. One SENCO shared how they brought in a consultant to help develop strategies for building relationships with 'hard-to-reach families'. The key learning from this experience:

> The families were not hard to reach, the school was hard to access.

## Box 4.2  Taking a pupil off the SEND register

From a primary school SENCO:

> I had a little girl in year one who had been a bit of a late starter. She had English as an additional language and her family didn't really have any experience of the English school system. She was delayed in her learning and also socially.

> She was on the SEND register with MLD as her main type of need, but she had an amazing year one teacher who got her back up to age-related [expectation]. As the SENCO, I could see that she no longer needed to be on the SEND register.

> I told the Headteacher I was planning to take her off the SEND register and she just looked at me blankly. She said, 'we never take children off the SEND register. SEND doesn't just disappear.'

> I was furious. Why block up provision for those who need it now with those who no longer need it? It makes no damn sense. And it's all contextual anyway. Our school was in quite a deprived area, so we would have children not on our SEND register that definitely would be if they were in a school in a less disadvantaged area. Isn't SEND a relative thing?

### Reflection Questions

1. Some SENCOs routinely place pupils on their 'watch list' if they come off the SEND register. What else could or should be put into place to ensure such a change is successful?
2. Is SEND always a relative concept? What message does it send to pupils with SEND and their families if they are taken off the SEND register?

## *Going the Extra Mile*

One of the most rewarding aspects of the role for some SENCOs was when they went the extra mile to fight for something they believed in and it paid off. One SENCO talked about how they 'put their neck on the line' for a pupil with SEND who they did not think was being given a fair chance. Over multiple years, the SENCO was a constant advocate for the pupil even when some members of the senior leadership team felt the pupil needed to be at a different school and were pushing for exclusion or a managed move. The SENCO kept the pupil at the school, and when they left with nine GCSEs, they felt it had all been worth it.

Another SENCO talked about a child in reception with cerebral palsy, who was wheelchair reliant for most of the time. She was a looked-after child and had an EHC plan. The SENCO was aware that the school would need to make adjustments to meet the girl's needs, including physical adjustments to the building. Whilst the school was ready to proceed, the Trust decided the adjustments were too expensive and consequently said they could not meet need. It became a Trust decision rather than a school decision. The SENCO argued the case strongly, including meeting with the Trust CEO. Eventually, it was agreed that the girl could remain at the school, and one of the key arguments from the SENCO was that anybody at the school could be involved in a car accident tomorrow, end up in a wheelchair and the Trust would need to make the adjustments anyway. The SENCO felt a huge sense of pride with this achievement.

When thinking about how to go the extra mile when resources are limited, one SENCO explained how it is about making the most of what you have got, rather than thinking about what you have not got. They suggested changing perspective and adapting to make the best of the situation you are in. They emphasised that

*inclusion is a journey, not a destination.*

---

### Box 4.3 Passion and politeness are not mutually exclusive

From a secondary school SENCO:

> I received a big ranting email from a parent about a maths teacher. It wasn't personal, but it was just about things that were happening in his class. Normally I would have picked out the relevant parts of the email and shared those with the specific teacher rather than sharing the whole email.

> But on this particular day, I was swamped. I was so busy. So, I just forwarded the email to the maths teacher and he got really upset. He talked about going to his Union. I couldn't understand why he was so upset. I was thinking 'that's just a normal email, like the kind I receive every day'.

> This incident shifted my perspective to think it's not okay for parents or anybody to speak to people in a rude away. The truth is that the SENCO role had desensitised me because I was seeing this stuff all the time.

> In some ways, being exposed to these emails was a good thing because it helped me to be resilient, but what it didn't help me to do was to have clear boundaries and expectations.

> Of course, I still get these types of emails, but now I try to be clear if things are not acceptable. I remind myself that parents are only being passionate about their child. But being passionate and polite can happen at the same time.

**Reflection Questions**

1. If a SENCO receives an email from a parent or a colleague that they deem to be impolite or aggressive, what steps should they take?
2. What proactive measures can schools put in place to support SENCOs with managing their workload?

## The Toll of the SENCO Role

The nature of the SENCO role is such that it can be physically, mentally and emotionally draining. Over time, SENCOs have developed many different methods and techniques for dealing with the demands of the role, and this is one the areas explored during the SENCO interviews.

### Leaning on Family and Colleagues

The vast majority of SENCOs talked about how their family and colleagues supported them through tough times. A few mentioned that they received support from close friends, but this was a minority, with most SENCOs feeling that the sensitive nature of much of their work limited the support they could receive from family, colleagues or very close friends. Here are some of the comments relating to emotional support that SENCOs received from their families:

> I have a lovely, supportive husband who would give me space when I had a bad day.

> When you do have those down moments, I'm lucky that my family are all in education so I can offload and they understand. Then you have to turn that negativity into productivity. I think, 'What's the next step? How are we going to do this?'

> I'm quite lucky that I'm not a very up and down person. Even if I've embarrassed myself by doing something silly, I try not to let it get to me, but sometimes you can't help it. Once, I had a SEND/safeguarding incident and I couldn't get over it all weekend. My poor husband basically allowed me to talk to him for the whole weekend about it. And then you start to worry that you are passing your stress onto others around you. I've also got a really good friend I can talk to, but there should be something built into the role really, like clinical supervision.

SENCOs were clear that they valued the support they received from their colleagues. Some described a sort of 'black humour' that existed amongst colleagues, where if they couldn't find a way to laugh about certain situations, then they would have to weep. Many SENCOs talked about the great support team they had around them in school who they felt they could talk to at any time. One SENCO from a special school explained that they had a standing agenda item as part of their leadership team meetings where people could 'get things off their chest'. It was described as 'a ten-minute slot for anybody to talk about the things that are majorly frustrating us or making us angry or upset'.

### Professional Support and Clinical Supervision

Around 10% of SENCOs interviewed indicated they had access to professional support or clinical supervision. One SENCO shared that they had clinical supervision and the end of each term as they found this was often the point at which stress had built up over time. In this particular case, the SENCO was also the DSL, and it was the DSL aspect of the role that allowed her to access the clinical supervision rather than the SENCO role in its own right.

Another SENCO who accessed clinical supervision fortnightly explained that there was buy-in from senior leaders at the school to support the wellbeing of staff. In this school, clinical supervision was in place for the SENCO, but it was also available to the learning mentor.

A different SENCO who accessed clinical supervision made it clear this was important because they were concerned about the potential transference of negative emotions from them to their family should this not be available. They shared how they had to fight for clinical supervision and how they were frustrated that clinical supervision was routinely available to social workers and health professionals but not to SENCOs. They found this to be particularly frustrating given that education professionals are increasingly filling gaps from public services more broadly.

Lastly, there was a SENCO whose school took a slightly different approach by appointing a clinical psychologist to work with them. In addition to providing clinical supervision, the psychologist helped the SENCO to develop a range of techniques to help them manage the emotional toll of the role. For example, the SENCO learnt neuro-linguistic programming methods such as anchoring and reframing. The SENCO described how these techniques became embedded in her day-to-day practice.

---

### Box 4.4 Trauma-informed approaches to SEND provision

From a special school SENCO:

> We had a particularly distressing situation with a boy who had a difficult family background. There were some mental health difficulties within the immediate family and the boy was struggling at school. He had an autism diagnosis and he was self-harming.

> The boy ended up blinding himself in one eye because and had to have state-of-the-art surgery to save his eye. He was required to wear an eye patch to help with the healing process, but there were concerns from the family about what other pupils might say.

> The boy stopped wearing the eye patch and sadly this affected the surgery that had been done. He went on to blind himself permanently.

### Reflection Questions

1. When SENCOs are dealing with situations involving self-harm, what therapeutic or trauma-informed approaches should they consider?
2. For situations spanning education, health and social care, how do SENCOs ensure they get the full participation of the family and other professionals?

---

### *Mindset*

Lots of SENCOs talked about the importance of having the right mindset to deal with the 'emotional rollercoaster' of the role.

> I deal with it by knowing that eventually there will be a high. There will always be a high with every child, so remember this when it gets demanding and it gets really upsetting. Because there will be highs. There will be moments when you realise that you're making a difference. If you've tried seven or eight things that haven't worked, you just have to keep going because it may well be the ninth thing that makes that difference. Remembering that will keep you going through the tough times.

Lots of SENCOs talked about using exercise to help them to maintain a positive mindset. Some go to the gym, whilst others do swimming or walking. Yoga and running were also mentioned regularly.

---

### Box 4.5 Intervening to prevent the self-fulfilling prophecy

From a primary school SENCO:

> I try to help other staff to prevent them creating a self-fulfilling prophecy. If I overhear a member of staff saying, 'Oh, my goodness, you've got him next year. Oh, you're really going to struggle', then I intervene because otherwise all they will know is negativity.

> That can really bring you down and actually convincing those staff that have heard those things that it's going be OK is part of the SENCO role in my opinion.

> That child might not have got on with Mrs X this year. But you're a different teacher; you're a different person. It's a different space and actually you might be the key to unlock that child.

## Reflection Questions

1. What options does a SENCO have in how they can intervene if staff are making inappropriate assumptions about pupils with SEND?
2. What systemic changes can school leaders make to promote a strengths-based culture within a school?

### *The SENCO Work-Life Balance*

Managing the work-life balance was a familiar issue for the vast majority of SENCOs, but very few felt they had found a solution they were 100% happy with. However, they did share plenty of good advice for those SENCOs struggling with workload demands.

To begin with, SENCOs felt there had to be an acknowledgement that there would always be more work to do. This is important because it indicates that a line between work-life and home-life must be drawn somewhere. Interestingly, the acknowledgement referred to here was more a self-acknowledgement than anything else, since it was generally SENCOs themselves who felt they needed to work longer hours rather than pressure from school leaders or families. When pressed on this, it was clear that SENCOs cared profoundly about their work and therefore wanted to do their utmost for the pupils with SEND for whom they were responsible.

One of the SENCOs admitted that they had become unwell whilst they were the SENCO in a previous school from not having a healthy work-life balance. They felt they 'learned the hard way' that they had to get it right. This SENCO was off work with stress for six months, and she felt incredibly guilty that she could not help any pupils at all during that period. She is now back in the SENCO role and has a new philosophy which centres on self-care. Using the analogy of the oxygen masks on an aeroplane, she described how it is important to look after yourself first and foremost so that you are in the best shape possible to do your best for others.

A common theme amongst SENCOs who had been in the role for more than five years was trying hard not to bring work home. There were lots of examples of SENCOs getting into school as early as 7 am and leaving as late as 6 pm so they could keep a clear divide and not let their work-life bleed into their home-life. However, when pressed further, it became apparent that this was an ambition, rather than a constant reality, as there were plenty of exceptions to the rule. For example, a few SENCOs talked about 'checking their schedule for the week' on Sunday evening to ensure everything was ready. Sometimes, this required some work to be done on a Sunday evening. One SENCO said they 'switched off completely from school whilst at home', but went on to say that they 'never switched off from safeguarding or child protection', adding that they routinely attend meetings during the holiday period.

> Of course, you do have to take work home sometimes. But I try to fit it all into my working week if at all possible. In practice, this means I need to be shut away, because if I'm sat here at this desk, people will just keep going past and putting their head round and it's 'just a quick one'.

> I can't really turn staff or pupils away. And of course it's never really a quick one, is it? It's always something quite complicated. They think it's simple though. They expect me to have a silver bullet and a solution in just one sentence . . . come on!

---

### Box 4.6  Appointing a Deputy SENCO

From a secondary school SENCO:

> As part of my SENCO role, I am a member of the senior leadership team at the school. This brings with it some other responsibilities, such as a lot of meetings. But to be fair, I now also have a Deputy SENCO. But that's a double edged-sword when it comes to work-life balance.

> I'm finding it hard not to micro-manage. Sometimes, I know I can do the tasks better, because I've done them so many times before, but I also know that I have to let him learn and make some mistakes. But I keep thinking that we are talking about real children and their lives. Mistakes aren't really an option. Part of it is that I feel like it might reflect badly on me if mistakes are made or if provision is not as good as it could be.

> On the plus side, I am now much more strategic in my role. I've had time to write the SEN strategy, which somebody else would have written before. That is helping me to influence SEND in a whole school way. It's an investment that should see bigger and better rewards over time.

### Reflection Questions

1. What lessons can SENCOs learn from the medical profession about effective practices in upskilling Deputy SENCOs, minimising mistakes and maximising delivery assurance?
2. Does having a Deputy SENCO help with workload by spreading it across two people, or does it increase workload as colleagues see there is now more capacity available?

---

Another recurring theme from SENCOs related to emails, or in the words of one SENCO, 'the never-ending flow of emails that come in at all hours of the day and night'. Experienced SENCOs were clear that they do not have their work emails on their mobile phone because this makes it impossible to switch off.

One SENCO made the point that it was as much about the notifications as it was about the emails themselves. She explained that once you receive the notification, there is a temptation to look. Then once you look, 'it is going around your head all evening and in the middle of the night, then you can't sleep'. Another SENCO said how he had made the mistake of replying to an email from a parent at 11 pm, which then created the expectation that he would always be on hand to respond that quickly and at that time of night.

SENCOs who were newer to the role were broadly divided into two clear groups when it came to managing workload and work-life balance. In one group, there were SENCOs who had clear expectations about working hours, with one stating:

> If the SENCO role cannot fit around my home life, then I will find another job. It is the Headteacher's responsibility to ensure this happens. I will not work in any job where my own health is compromised for work.

In the second group, the opposite was true. SENCOs accepted that the role was 'a lifestyle choice' or 'part of your DNA'. One suggested that being the SENCO was 'not a job, but a way of life'. This group of SENCOs appeared to have bought into the notion that the SENCO role demands a more flexible and pragmatic approach with blurry edges between work-life and home-life. One SENCO explained it like this:

> I'm not the best one to ask about work-life balance because I'm not very good at it. If there's stuff to be done, I will sit and do it. The only thing I can do to justify that with myself is that I'm very lucky that I get the holidays that I get and so I will spend all the term-time working evenings and working one day a week during the weekend and I will keep going.

> But then during half term and Christmas and all that, I shut off. Well, I'm never properly switched off, but mostly switched off. I don't think there's a point in switching off completely. I mean, I've got 39 children on my caseload.

Now they're not all going through my brain all the time, but some of them are. There are certain few children that are constantly ticking through your head all the time. What's my next step? What do I need to do? How can I fight for this? How can I get more for that? It's constant.

## Relationships

Maintaining positive relationships with a broad range of stakeholders is a key aspect of the SENCO role. This includes parents, colleagues, professionals from external services and pupils. The context in which these relationships need to be managed is often fraught with tension and adversarial in nature due to regular mismatches between stakeholder expectations and the resource constraints of the system.

Despite these challenges, SENCOs are often the lynchpin of effective relationships. Somehow they regularly manage to sufficiently satisfy a diverse set of stakeholders who, on the face of it, have competing sets of needs and expectations. This sub-section seeks to uncover some of the SENCO secrets that help them to achieve this.

### *Relationships in General*

During the interviews, SENCOs were clear that part of what they do is just about treating everybody that they meet as decent people who have good intentions. Whilst it may seem at first that others want something different than you, it is often the case that there is a common purpose. Often, this commonality is that everybody wants to put quality provision in place for those who need it, which is not a bad place to start. As one SENCO put it:

> People don't get up in the morning and go to work with the express intention of giving a bad deal to children with SEND. That just doesn't happen.

SENCOs outlined a range of strategies they use during meetings, such as always asking people how they are and thanking people even if they cannot help you. They described how it was important to 'cut people slack when they need it' and to 'speak to people in a respectful way like I would want to be spoken to'.

One SENCO talked about allowing parents and professionals from external services to be more knowledgeable than them as the SENCO. They made the point that demonstrating some knowledge as a SENCO can be reassuring, but too much can be counterproductive. The SENCO argued that this approach helped parents to feel more in control, thereby maximising their contribution to a coproduced solution. For professionals, the SENCO argued that demonstrating too much knowledge made them question whether they were adding value, so they might focus their efforts elsewhere.

Another key message from SENCOs was to be patient with colleagues or with parents if they made choices that made the situation worse, rather than making it better. Returning to the principle of good intentions, several SENCOs suggested it was important to be pragmatic and to forgive mistakes quickly without attributing blame. In the words of one SENCO:

> When people make the wrong choices, it is almost certainly through ignorance, not negligence If they get it wrong, you shouldn't get it wrong too by blaming them.

### *Relationships with Parents and Carers*

When it comes to engagement with parents and carers, SENCOs were clear that honesty is the best policy. One SENCO explained that early in their career, their line manager, who was the Deputy Headteacher, had advised that the best way to deal with all parental requests for additional support was to say it would take time to collate the evidence. The SENCO pointed out that the issue here was not about evidence, but that this tactic was being used to delay provision going into place to save money. The SENCO did not approve of this approach and eventually changed schools.

Most SENCOs were consistent in their view that their professional opinion based on experience and expertise should be shared from the outset. This helps with managing expectations, but also in setting out a clear way forwards agreed by all. It was also common for SENCOs to want to be involved in meetings between the class teacher and the parents of pupils with SEND to help build strong, multi-dimensional relationships.

> I think that you try very hard not to promise parents more than you can deliver. And if you do say you're going to do something by a certain time, you try extremely hard to get it done by that time. If something can't be done, be honest about it from the outset.

Almost all of the SENCOs interviewed explicitly vocalised the important role of parents and carers as equal, meaningful partners in coproducing effective SEND provision. Families will have developed ways of working that are known to work and that can be replicated in school. For those joining early years settings, it may also be that the family have been the main educator up until this point.

One the challenges commonly experienced by SENCOs in relation to parents was when there was denial about the needs of the child. There were different reasons for such denials, including cultural norms or religious beliefs, but convincing some parents and carers to accept that their child had SEND and would benefit from additional support was hard. SENCOs described having to respond to parental comments such as 'he will grow out of it' or 'she will be fine – I was the same at school'.

One SENCO shared an interesting use of AI in helping her to improve how she communicates with families. For this SENCO, most of her meetings are video calls held on Microsoft Teams. With the permission of the parents and carers on the call, she records the meetings. This is partly because she uses the built-in transcription function as a written record of the meeting. However, she also uses AI sentiment analysis to assess her communication style and how parents and carers are responding to her. The AI then provides feedback and suggestions as to how she can improve her communication in the future. This is a novel approach to using AI, and it will be interesting if such techniques become more commonplace as the technology becomes more readily available in schools.

A significant minority of SENCOs referred to the challenge of local authorities routinely refusing requests for EHC needs assessments, claiming 'more cycles evidence of the graduated approach' were needed. This is relevant to effective relationships with families as these SENCOs observed that there were typically fewer hurdles and evidence requirements when the same requests for an EHC needs assessments were submitted by parents or carers. This echoes the findings of a recent study on the 'coproduction illusion', which is discussed further at the end of this chapter (Boddison and Soan, 2021).

## Relationships with Colleagues

SENCOs were generally optimistic about their relationships with other colleagues at their schools. In some instances, the Headteacher was a former SENCO or was a vocal advocate of inclusion, which SENCOs believed was helpful in setting the right culture for relationships to flourish.

SENCOs were consistently inconsistent when outlining the extent to which their teaching colleagues were advocates of SEND and inclusion. In no instances did a SENCO report that every single member of teaching staff in their school was a full advocate of SEND and inclusion all of the time. In practice, SEND advocacy seemed to vary from person to person and depended on individual workload and other time pressures. In some instances, SENCOs reported that teachers still saw SEND as being somebody else's responsibility once a certain threshold of volume or complexity of need had been reached.

> Remember that not every member of staff that you deal with is going to be as passionate about children with SEND as you are. It's going to be about supporting and showing staff what can be done if even just a few little things are put in place.

---

**Box 4.7  Is the EHC plan a 'golden ticket'?**

From a primary school SENCO:

> Sometimes, when teachers or parents are knocking on your door saying we need a referral for this, we need a referral for that, for the benefit of the child and relationship, the SENCO must be honest with them.

> The problem is that they believe that the piece of paper (EHC plan) will be the key to everything. 'Let's get a referral. Let's get them seen.'

> They believe the piece of paper that comes through is going to fix everything – like some kind of golden ticket. And then they're bitterly disappointed when the piece of paper that comes through is actually just saying the stuff that we've been doing already. And there's nothing new on it.

> So it's about helping them to understand that coming to me for a referral is not a magic wand. It's not necessarily going to do anything unless the needs are significant because what we've already got in place for that child is what we would have put in place for that child anyway.

> It's like if we get a letter from an EP saying that their child has ADHD, they think that everything is magically fixed now. They say, 'right, we've got this letter, so what you're going to do?' and I have to sit there and say that we can't do any more than we are doing already.

**Reflection Questions**

1. In making the judgement about whether or not to request a needs assessment to secure an EHC plan, what factors should be taken into consideration?
2. If the provision outlined in an EHC plan describes the existing provision that is already in place for a child, what is its value and purpose?

---

## SENCOs and Ofsted Inspections

### *Data and the Big Picture*

When it comes to Ofsted inspections, the SENCOs interviewed had a wealth of combined experience that they were willing to share. This started with ensuring that your knowledge goes beyond individual pupils and that as the SENCO you understand the trends in the data and the big picture.

Lots of SENCOs talked about the importance of being able to articulate clearly and concisely where the school is on its SEND journey. This was about celebrating the successes of the journey, but also the challenges and what is in place to address those challenges. SENCOs explained that having an in-depth understanding of how the school is set up in terms of provision and staffing is useful as it shows how different aspects of the school offer come together to meet different types of need.

When it comes to data, SENCOs echoed the expectations set out in the SEND Code of Practice (DfE and DoH, 2015), which is that there should be comparisons to local and national averages with some analysis of what this means for your school. One SENCO explained how they like to also separate out the data into the four broad areas of need. They used this data to provide nuance in the SEND conversation and to articulate where the school was making an impact and where it was still developing its approach.

Data on the impact of interventions was raised frequently by SENCOs. This went beyond the impact of interventions for specific pupils and was instead focused on the quality of the interventions more broadly. Several SENCOs described being asked by Ofsted inspectors questions akin to the following:

- What is your most impactful intervention? How do you know?
- What processes and procedures do you have in place to monitor the impact of interventions?
- What role does 'value for money' play when selecting interventions for pupils with SEND?

## *Case Studies*

There was general agreement from SENCOs that having some case studies to demonstrate the impact of SEND provision was helpful.

> Have a couple of case studies that you can talk through immediately to show evidence that interventions are making a difference to individual children.
>
> In my experience, Ofsted inspectors will quite happily sit and look at the bigger picture through the data, but what you can do is bring that data to life through the use of some real-life case studies to personalise the data.

---

### Box 4.8 Celebrating the small things (which are also the big things!)

From a special school SENCO:

> We had a girl with Developmental Language Disorder (DLD) and her parents were in denial about that in year one, even though she was in a special school. They kept saying she would be back in mainstream school soon and that this was only a temporary situation.
>
> Finally in year two, working very closely with mum and building a more trusting relationship, they came round to it. Basically, she couldn't read at all in year two. With some intensive interventions over the next year she learned four sounds. That was it.
>
> It sounds small I know, but I was like 'this is huge progress!' Its' important to celebrate the small things, which are really big things if we are honest with ourselves.'

### Reflection Questions

1. In a world where 'age-related expectations' dominate the educational landscape for primary-aged children, how should SENCOs approach the conversation about celebrating small steps of progress with an Ofsted inspector?
2. What lessons can SENCOs in primary schools learn from SENCOs in special schools about tracking and monitoring small steps of progress?

---

## *Practical Advice*

There was lots of practical advice for SENCOs, which was based on their previous experience of Ofsted inspections. Much of it is common sense, but even one thing that a SENCO does differently during an inspection could make all the difference.

> Think carefully before you answer any questions. Just be reflective and if you don't understand the question, ask for clarification.

> It is foolish to let your mouth run away with you. You're better to say less and say it well, than to say more that is mediocre.

> If you struggle with the data side of things, then get a data-savvy colleague to give you a data briefing and a crib sheet before you talk to Ofsted. Get them to ask you questions on the data, so you have a dry run.

When Ofsted talked to me, they wanted me to walk them around the school and to take them into lessons to point out very specifically how the needs of learners with SEND were being met. This is where the governor learning walks we had done proved invaluable.

On my inspection, it was all about individual children. They asked 'Why did this child get this grade when his target was this grade? Does this mean the provision was ineffective?' So, it's important to be able to discuss individual children and the needs they have as well as the big picture.

Make sure your provision map is bang up to date.

When they [Ofsted] go into classrooms, make sure that they can see that it's not always a teaching assistant that's interacting with your high needs children. Those children should also have as much input from the teacher as other pupils, maybe more. Because obviously children with SEND need the highest qualified professionals, don't they? With Ofsted, point out explicitly where this is happening.

Be clear about what teachers are doing about meeting needs in the classroom. That's a question I've had in my past three inspections. They say the work of the SENCO is all fine, but how do you know that teachers are being inclusive in the classroom?

## Good Intentions

One of the more sombre moments within the interviews with SENCOs was when they were asked for their reflections on instances where they had good intentions but things did not turn out as planned. Such instances were clearly a source of frustration for SENCOs, not least because it is clear they really want to secure the best possible provision for pupils with SEND.

There have been times when I've really wanted something for a child. For example, one child needed to have respite provision, but I was not able to make it happen. You know, school just can't make it happen, and that's frustrating. But the parents don't tend to blame you because they know that that's out of your control. But I hate that part of the job.

I try to have amazing relationships with all the families, but sometimes it just doesn't work out. We had one dad who was really difficult, despite my efforts for him. The problem was that if he didn't get his own way on everything, he would just keep going to the next person until he got the answer he wanted. There would be a conversation with the class teacher, then me, then the head teacher. In hindsight, we should have tried to direct him to one person as a key contact, but I'm not sure he would have listened. We really did try to do our best.

One SENCO described a situation where they had managed to secure some support from an occupational therapist for a child. This took months of work, but the family disagreed with the approach and put in a formal complaint to the school. It ended up being a protracted conversation that governors got involved with, and the SENCO explained that the relationship was never the same again after that point. There was a feeling that trust had been broken, despite the best efforts of the SENCO.

---

**Box 4.9 Behaviour as a communication of need**

From a primary school SENCO:

There was one teacher at our school who was an early-career teacher (ECT). She prepared her classroom for the start of term and it was a beautiful classroom. It was absolutely stunning. They'd been to Ikea and really gone to town. Everything matched. Everything was lovely, typical of what you'd expect from an ECT.

Within three or four weeks, there was one boy who regularly became dysregulated in the classroom. But the teacher cared a lot and she tried everything she could think of to help him. She was wonderfully patient and kind, but nothing she did was working.

She came to me as the SENCO for advice and we looked at everything. We looked for patterns. We thought about what was happening at home and at school. We thought about what the triggers might be. Was the behaviour in certain lessons or at certain times of day? We did absolutely everything we could think of, but for three months this behaviour carried on and the classroom ended up getting wrecked.

It turned out that the teacher had put the most beautiful rug in this boy's workspace and it was the texture of the rug was what was setting him off. It took us absolutely ages to figure this out. It wasn't until he stood up with a tub of PVA glue and poured it all over the rug. The teacher had to get rid of the rug and it was then that we realised the rug was to blame as once this was gone the behaviour changed.

By this time, the teacher was at the end of her tether and she had already gone to the Headteacher to say she couldn't teach this boy anymore and that she was concerned about the impact on other children in the class.

I had to intervene as the SENCO to keep the child in school. Once we knew it was a sensory issue, we looked at other potential sensory triggers too. The teacher had a lot on their display boards. It was just too much, and he wasn't able to cope with it. And as soon as we stripped his whole area back to being very simple, everything was fine. Of course, he did have a few moments of challenging behaviour, but on the whole the problem was pretty much solved.

## Reflection Questions

1. How should SENCOs convince those who believe in zero-tolerance behaviour policies that behaviour is a communication of need rather than deliberate defiance?
2. When it comes to sensory needs, some children crave sensory stimulation, whilst others can be overwhelmed by sensory stimulation. In a class with a diverse range of sensory needs, what is the right approach for teachers to take?

## Conclusion

This chapter has shared a range of insights from SENCOs, from those things they feel have been career successes to those things which have been professionally challenging. In either case, there are lessons here that can be learned by SENCOs more generally. However, learning lessons is insufficient; it is applying the learning from those lessons where real change occurs.

## Reflection Questions

1. What learning have you taken from the SENCO experiences shared in this chapter? How will you apply this learning to your professional practice?
2. How might a school go about routinely collating lessons learned from its stakeholders to feed into a cycle of continuous improvement?

## Suggested Resources

1. University College London (UCL) Centre for Inclusive Education has published guidance on professional supervision for school leaders and SENCOs (Carroll et al., 2020). This guidance explains the different types of professional supervision and how these can be useful for SENCOs and school leaders. https://discovery.ucl.ac.uk/id/eprint/10090818/1/Carroll_SENCO%20Supervision%20Guidance%20 February%202020.pdf
2. The *Coproduction Illusion* (Boddison and Soan, 2021) is a study that compares the relative success and efficiency rates for EHC plans when requested by parents and carers or by education professionals. https://nasenjournals.onlinelibrary.wiley.com/doi/abs/10.1111/1471-3802.12545

# 5 Individual Stories

## Bobby

### Background and Context

Bobby was the second child born in his family. His older sibling was an adult but still lived in the family home. Bobby's parents were never together during his lifetime, but his mum had a support network including her brother and the wider family community who lived nearby. Bobby grew up in an area of high deprivation and crime, and he spent lots of time in the local community.

Bobby attended the local primary school, where he joined them from foundation stage two (the reception year). There were no major concerns, but it was noted that Bobby had not made a friend or engaged in play other than solitary play. Bobby's mum struggled to get him to wear his uniform or to get him into a routine for school. As a result, his attendance was sporadic, and this was not regularly followed up by the school.

When Bobby started year one, other difficulties began to emerge. He struggled following instructions and engaging in group tasks. In particular, Bobby did not cope well with any staffing changes. Initially Bobby's avoidance was passive, and he would not engage at all, but over time Bobby's mum had more and more difficulties getting him into school. He began to be aggressive towards his mother when she tried to implement bedtime or other routines or to get him ready for school. As a result, his mother began avoiding school routines, and his attendance dipped to below 50%.

When the pressure and demands increased in the classroom, Bobby's behaviour became more challenging still. For example, he would run out of the classroom and throw tables and chairs at staff. This cycle continued to increase in pressure over the first term of year one, and by the end of this term Bobby had had three fixed-term exclusions.

Moving into term two, the behaviours escalated further both at home and at school. Bobby began biting his mother and physically attacking her multiple times a day. In school, Bobby was now attacking children and staff every time he was in the building, resulting in a string of further suspensions.

### Responses Over Time

The school started withdrawing Bobby from his lessons for one-to-one sessions on anger management. However, he did all he could to avoid attending these sessions. Eventually, the SENCO felt the demand added to days that were already difficult and stressful for Bobby. The school appointed a teaching assistant to work with Bobby on a one-to-one basis to manage his time at school, but despite this use of targeted resource, there was limited success or change.

The school requested an assessment with the aim of securing an EHC plan for Bobby. The relationship between home and school was frayed. Bobby's mum was being physically abused at home, and she was being regularly invited into meetings that felt damning and shaming. Bobby's mum stopped answering the phone when the school called because the home situation was so negative and difficult at this time.

At the start of term three, Bobby came to school and was having a good day. He was at lunch with other pupils in his class when he picked up a knife and pointed it towards another 5-year-old due to a disagreement on the lunch table. Staff quickly took the knife away from him, but he was permanently excluded for this incident.

### Bobby's New School

Bobby's EHC plan was finalised, and he was allocated a place at an SEMH school. Bobby and his mum came to look around the school and were feeling positive about the move. However,

DOI: 10.4324/9781032634807-5

when it came to his first day, Bobby's mum struggled to get him into school. She spoke to the family support at the school and was encouraged to bring him any time during the day but not to give up. By the time they eventually arrived at the school, both Bobby and his mum were exhausted; and then Bobby attacked the staff at his new school.

For the first three days Bobby never made it to the classroom. Instead, much of his time was spent attacking the staff in the school and attacking his mum on the journey to school. During short periods of time when he was calm, he did complete some activities with the member of support staff in his class, Mrs Bay, and he began to build a relationship with her.

On day four, Bobby got up, got dressed and came to school with no issues. Bobby went to class and began to cry. Mrs Bay wondered out loud about how Bobby was feeling and soon came to the understanding that he was nervous about getting it wrong. Mrs Bay worked with him on a whiteboard, and Bobby copied this into his book. Bobby needed repeated reassurance throughout that day, but he managed to take part in all the lessons, and at the end of the day he asked to show his mum his work.

In the end, Bobby settled quickly into his new school. He found any time he left the classroom or any change of staff hard, but Mrs Bay recognised this and worked with him to develop strategies to show when he was worried or how he could get help. When it came to PE lessons, Bobby was not yet able to join in, but he stayed with his class and watched the session which he had agreed with staff in advance.

Fast forward into the future Bobby is happy at school and making good progress. He has 100% attendance, and Mum is now back at work with very few issues at home. On occasion, Bobby still gets overwhelmed, and he will show this through crying, and staff quickly respond by providing safe spaces and options to allow him to be successful.

### Reflections

When reflecting on this situation, it is worth considering the *boundary seesaw model* (Hamilton, 2010, pp. 184–185). This model suggests there are three distinct roles that can be adopted by those in positions of authority: the security guard, the super-carer or the mediator.

In Bobby's first school, it could be argued that the staff and Bobby's mum both took on a 'security guard' role. Consequently, it is perhaps not surprising that Bobby's behaviour was akin to that of being in a prison, where every rule feels like it is there to constrain you. Similarly, it could be argued that the staff also adopted a 'security guard' role as the basis of their relationship with Bobby's mum, which might explain why she became disengaged with the school.

When Bobby attended his new school, a more balanced approach was used (perhaps the 'mediator' role?). The use of firm boundaries and expectations alongside nurture to support him facilitated a balanced response from Bobby. This included an opportunity for him to express his emotions through crying rather than aggression.

## Harry

### Background and Context

Harry grew up in a city in the North of England within a loving family of two parents and an older sibling. He met all his early years milestones, but at the age of 3, his parents started to notice that he was finding some situations more difficult than his peers. There appeared to be a disparity between how Harry coped in larger or new social situations, particularly those which had not encountered before. During this time, Harry's parents managed any arising challenges successfully through careful planning and preparation. Sometimes, this involved leaving social situations early or, on occasion, avoiding situations altogether.

During reception, when Harry was age 5, his difficulties in regulating his emotions become more apparent. For example, there were situations in school where Harry would physically harm other children during his emotional outbursts. The school operated an 'end of the day check out' system, where parents would queue to collect their child and receive feedback on how their child had got on that day. Whilst this was done with good intentions, it felt like 'a bag of shame' was being handed over at the end of each day. The number of concerns about Harry's behaviours seemed to be growing every day, and the family also had to hear the reactions of other parents whose children had been on the receiving end of the emotional outbursts.

## *Lockdown*

Harry's parents began to notice patterns in the locations and times of the incidents. Issues were primarily occurring in places of high footfall (such as the cloakroom) or during of times of transition (such as in corridors or at break times). Before this could be explored further, the Covid-19 pandemic occurred, which impacted Harry's schooling and meant he was then at home for extended periods during the national lockdown.

The period of lockdown highlighted specific concerns for his parents, who have a professional background in SEND. They noticed Harry's inattentiveness even during one-to-one time with his parents. Harry had experienced anxiety about his work and about engaging online with staff and peers. This firmed up the concerns that his parents had, and so they began to consider ADHD as a possible reason for his difficulties. However, they were also acutely aware that a diagnosis would be in the future due to his young age and due to the disruption of the pandemic.

## *The Developing Relationship Between School and Home*

Year one followed a similar path to reception with Harry having comparable incidents, but spending more extended periods outside of the classroom with a teaching assistant. Harry's parents suspected that he preferred being outside the classroom and that he was behaving in a certain way to secure an exit from the classroom.

At the start of year two, there was some light at the end of the tunnel. Harry started to receive support from a very experienced teaching assistant who understood his needs. He felt cared for and safe whilst being given clear boundaries. There were still difficulties, but there were also far more settled times.

Sadly, Harry's dad passed away just before the Christmas holidays in year three. Harry and his family spent the next few weeks together grieving, and he returned to school after the natural break.

Reflecting back on this, his mum felt this had helped him as there was no pressure from the school allowing them to just be together as a family. The school went above and beyond to support and nurture the family at this time, with three members of school staff attending the funeral, including senior staff, his class teacher and the teaching assistant who had been supporting Harry. During the funeral Harry started to struggle, and he moved to be with his school staff who were well placed to support him.

This support continued back in school, with Harry's teaching assistant contacting a national bereavement charity and pulling together a set of resources, including books to share with him in school and books he could take home. Harry spent a lot of time outside the classroom creating a special memory book at this time.

The remainder of that Spring term had ups and downs for Harry, as one might expect given the grieving process compounded with the previous difficulties he had had in school. Nevertheless, the school continued to go the extra mile to support the whole family.

## *Escalation of Behaviours and Consequences*

A change in the leadership personnel at the school coincided with a change in Harry's behaviour. He became more violent than he had ever been, he was in a bigger body and curriculum expectations continued to grow. This is when Harry was first suspended from school, and such suspensions continued from this point forwards. Harry had now begun to really harm his peers physically, and situations began to become unmanageable even by those staff who had worked so well for him in the past.

Harry's mum did not challenge the suspension, recognising that the school had been continuously working closely with Harry and her. She reflected on the fact that in another school, such suspensions may have happened sooner and that Harry would potentially have been permanently excluded. Although there was understanding from the school about the various pressures on the family, the ongoing situation meant that Harry's mum was unable to work, so she remained at home to support Harry.

The next step was an agreement to implement a part-time timetable for Harry, which included aspects such as coming home for lunch or having shorter days where needed. Harry found this difficult and may well have perceived this as a rejection in the relationship. The part-time timetable did not have the intended impact, and Harry's behaviour escalated. There were daily episodes of running around school and damaging property. Harry presented more regularly as being angry with the adults around him. The school, Harry and his family were all experiencing immense pressure at this point. In another school, this may well have been the point at which the decision was made to permanently exclude.

## *A Different Approach*

Something had to change, and Harry's mum met with a senior leader at the school with whom she had worked closely and felt there was a level of trust in the relationship. Due to this strong relationship, Mum was able to be completely vulnerable and air difficult questions such as 'Will Harry see out this year?', 'Will he see out his time in a mainstream primary?', 'Is this the beginning of the end of his time here?'. The openness and transparency allowed for a genuine, collaborative conversation about the possibility of a mixed placement to help structure Harry's week differently.

Shortly after the meeting it was proposed by the school that Harry would spend a day in the middle of the week at a local forest school provision. This day was also the day he would have had different staff in school, which helped to ensure that the school aspect of his week became more consistent.

In the summer holiday before year four, Harry started medication for ADHD and began his split-week schooling. His impulsive behaviour reduced, and he became happier in general. The week became more achievable for everyone. At the time of writing, there have been long periods with no significant incidents or suspensions. Harry even won a prize for his learning for the first time ever in his school career.

## *Reflections*

When reflecting on this situation, it is worth considering the approach the school has taken from a relational perspective. Despite the challenging circumstances and ethical dilemmas, they brought Harry's mum with them along the journey and ensured she played a central role in making the key decisions.

The parental relationship with the school developed over time through collaborative working and coproduction. The school would likely argue that they had no option other than to suspend Harry when they did. You might consider whether the school had any alternative options to using exclusion.

## Mary, Zora, Clare, Savita, Zoey, Grey and Gracey

### *Background and Context*

In September 2020, seven pupils joined their new secondary school. This was during the global pandemic, and as such these pupils had no explicit end to their primary school journey. This particular secondary school is an academy with a high number of feeder schools across the city in which it is based.

In general, the transition into year seven can be tricky as it involves bringing together a group of children at very different points on the maturity curve. Some have started puberty; some are independent and street-wise; some are academically ready but not socially ready for the transition; some are still young, with the transition into secondary school being a huge step.

Year seven was a disjointed experience for the pupils due to multiple Covid outbreaks and lockdowns. Consequently, the pupils' integration into the school was stifled due to imposed limitations, such as the 'bubble system', which meant pupils had to remain within pre-determined groups.

It was clear from the outset that this group of seven pupils stood out as needing more support. For example, there were issues linked to social media and some bullying incidents.

However, due to their disjointed attendance and the context of a global pandemic, the usual strategies were not implemented or followed through.

The group consisted of seven children (Mary, Zora, Clare, Savita, Zoey, Grey and Gracey) who individually had multiple adverse childhood experiences (ACEs). Some of the pupils had parents who were in prison, and all were from single-parent families. There were also significant mental health needs amongst the parents/carers.

Leaders at the school reflected on the complexity of needs for this group of children and determined that the rigid approach was unlikely to work for them or for others in the school. The decision was made to implement a 'key worker approach', which for this group involved members of the leadership team being the key adult and contact for both the child and the family. More strategically, policies, processes and procedures were reviewed to make them more psychologically informed to align with the approach being taken.

### Mary

During years eight, nine and ten, Mary was involved in multiple low-level incidents, usually related to disputes with peers, social media and work avoidance. Mary followed this up with her key worker regularly and began to reflect more on her choices and responses. Before long, Mary began to see and understand others' positions and perspectives when they were different to her own.

At the end of year ten Mary's dad was released from prison, and she moved in with him. Mary bounced between her parents when her behaviour dipped. In practice, neither parent wanted to be responsible for supporting Mary with her behavioural difficulties, so she moved back and forth between them, often multiple times per week. This was problematic, not least because each parent had a different set of rules and expectations. Mary's behaviour then escalated in school to the point where she was attempting to sell drugs on site. In response, the school then exercised their power to permanently exclude her due to the risks the drugs had on the wider school community.

### Zora

Zora was arguably the main success story from the seven pupils. Zora had a number of physical altercations during her time in school. She was impulsive and had a strong sense of social justice. In the heat of the moment, Zora would often make an instant decision on how to resolve an incident and would then follow it through, irrespective of the potential consequences. Her key worker was often called upon to move her away from a dispute or away from a heightened situation.

With the help of her key worker, Zora did make it through to the end of year 11 at this school. Zora's family worked closely with the school to ensure there was alignment between the conversations that were happening at home and those that were happening in school. As far as possible, the school also sought to support Zora to deal with her difficult home situation.

Zora had a member of the leadership team as her key worker, and she used them to support her reflection on difficult situations in school. She struggled at the end of year 11 with a bullying incident, in which she was unable to see the other child's point of view and the potential legal consequences of her decisions and actions.

The school made the decision to let her sit her exams, but this had to be done off site. Even after this decision Zora wrote an email to the school sharing how much she loved them. During the period of time in the run-up to her exams and during them, staff visited her off site and provided one-to-one sessions with key staff as well as online sessions for work and individual leavers' celebrations with staff.

### The Other Children in the Group

The other children in the group (Savita, Zoey, Grey and Gracey) saw a significant reduction in incidents. The girls did still have fallouts within the group, but they were regularly sharing these with their key workers to resolve disputes in a healthy way. This was a group of individuals that school leaders would not have sought to put together from the outset as their behaviours would have been easier to manage individually. However, the circumstances of the lockdown have meant this was unavoidable, and they have been drawn together.

## *Reflections*

When reflecting on this situation, it is worth considering the views of the site manager who was the individual who ended up cleaning up graffiti and damage caused by this group on multiple occasion.

> I saw them all at the open evening and they've changed so much . . . they really have . . . they're not perfect. . . . Don't get me wrong. They're so much more pleasant just around and about when I encounter them. . . . I know them all by name.

## Conclusion

It is evident from the individual stories that situations can quickly become complex. In such circumstances, making the right choices is challenging, both ethically and emotionally. There are often competing expectations and perspectives, and it is almost always impossible to give everybody what they want.

When it comes to inclusion and exclusion, the stakes become higher still as these decisions are likely to have significant implications for the future of the young person concerned as well as of those around them. For education professionals in schools, the remit of the role is broadening out into health and social care. The edges of the education profession are arguably fuzzier than ever before. Nevertheless, as this book has shown, many SENCOs and school leaders continue to do all in their power to make a difference.

It is not sustainable for SENCOs to fight for everything and everyone, so they need to be selective on how they use their time and resources. SENCOs need to pick their battles. SENCOs should focus on those battles that are small enough to win but big enough to make a difference.

## Reflection Questions

1. When behaviour is challenging for you, where does it typically come from? Why is this more challenging for you than for others?
2. What is the importance of parental communications and relationships? What are the easy mistakes to make, and what are the quick wins?

## Suggested Resources

1. *Healthy relationships with ourselves and with our peers* is free resource aimed at secondary schools in the UK to improve the mental health literacy of pupils and to help them build and maintain healthy relationships. It includes lesson plans, work sheets, presentations, an assembly plan, posters and guides. www.mentalhealth.org.uk/our-work/public-engagement/healthy-relationships/healthy-relationships-ourselves-and-our-peers-schools-pack
2. This seminar hosted by *Genuine Partnerships* and published by the *Council for Disabled Children* discusses coproduction, engagement and empowerment. https://councilfordisabledchildren.org.uk/about-us-0/networks/early-years-send/early-years-send-partnership-resources/co-production

# Glossary of Acronyms

| | |
|---|---|
| **ACE** | Adverse Childhood Experience |
| **ADHD** | Attention-Deficit Hyperactivity Disorder |
| **AI** | Artificial Intelligence |
| **ARC** | Attachment Research Community |
| **ARE** | Age-Related Expectation |
| **ASD** | Autism Spectrum Disorder |
| **BRAG** | Blue, Red, Amber, Green |
| **CAMHS** | Child and Adolescent Mental Health Services |
| **CEO** | Chief Executive Officer |
| **CMCAFS** | Changing Minds Child and Family Services |
| **CPD** | Continuing Professional Development |
| **C&I** | Communication and Interaction |
| **C&L** | Cognition and Learning |
| **DEIB** | Diversity, Equity, Inclusion and Belonging |
| **DfE** | Department for Education |
| **DLD** | Developmental Language Disorder |
| **DoH** | Department for Health |
| **DSL** | Designated Safeguarding Lead |
| **EAL** | English as an Additional Language |
| **EBD** | Education and Behavioural Difficulties |
| **ECT** | Early Career Teacher |
| **EDI** | Equity (equality), Diversity and Inclusion |
| **EHC plan** | Education, Health and Care plan |
| **EP** | Educational Psychologist |
| **GCSE** | General Certificate of Secondary Education |
| **HEART** | Holistic Thinking, Empowering the School Community, Aspirations for All Pupils, Relational Focus, Trust and Safety |
| **IEP** | Individual Education Plan |
| **IFS** | Institute for Fiscal Studies |
| **JCQ** | Joint Council for Qualifications |
| **LA** | Local Authority |
| **LAC** | Looked-After Children |
| **LLM** | Large Language Model |
| **MLD** | Moderate Learning Difficulties |
| **nasen** | National Association for Special Educational Needs |
| **NHS** | National Health Service |
| **NPQ** | National Professional Qualification |
| **OBE** | Officer of the Order of the British Empire |
| **ODI** | Open Data Institute |
| **ONS** | Office for National Statistics |
| **OT** | Occupational Therapist |
| **PACE** | Playfulness, Acceptance, Curiosity and Empathy |
| **PE** | Physical Education |
| **QFT** | Quality-First Teaching |
| **RACI** | Responsible, Accountable, Consulted/Coproduced, Informed |
| **RAG** | Red, Amber, Green |
| **SaLT** | Speech and Language Therapist |
| **SEMH** | Social, Emotional, Mental Health |
| **SEN** | Special Educational Needs |
| **SENCO** | Special Educational Needs Coordinator |
| **SEND** | Special Educational Needs and/or Disabilities |

| | |
|---|---|
| **SLCN** | Speech, Language and Communication Needs |
| **TA** | Teaching Assistant |
| **TD** | Typically Developing |
| **TES** | Times Education Supplement |
| **TTA** | Teacher Training Agency |
| **UCL** | University College London |
| **WSS** | Whole School SEND |
| **4Rs** | Regulate, Relate, Reason, Repair |

# References

Algraigray, H. and Boyle, C. (2017) The SEN label and its effect on special education. *Educational and Child Psychology*, Vol. 34, No. 4, pp. 70–89.

Aubin, G. (2022) Hidden at the whole-class level. *SEND Matters*. https://sendmatters.co.uk/2022/12/20/hidden-at-the-whole-class-level/ Accessed in December 2023.

Beere, J. (2014) Foreword. In Packer, N. (ed.) *The Perfect SENCO*. Carmarthen: Independent Thinking Press.

Biklen, D., Bogdan, R. and Blatt, B. (1979) Label jars, not people. In Harmony, M. (ed.) *Promise and Performance: ACT's Guide to TV Programming for Children*. Cambridge, MA: Ballinger.

Boddison, A. (2018) SEND leadership. In Bartram, D. (ed.) *Great Expectations: Leading an Effective SEND Strategy in School*. Woodbridge: John Catt.

Boddison, A. (2019a) Does Ofsted's draft inspection framework pass the inclusion test? *Schools Week*. https://schoolsweek.co.uk/does-ofsteds-draft-inspection-framework-pass-the-inclusion-test/ Accessed in December 2023.

Boddison, A. (2019b) Foreword. In Webster, R. (ed.) *Including Children and Young People with Special Educational Needs and Disabilities in Learning and Life*. Oxon: Routledge.

Boddison, A. (2021) *The Governance Handbook for SEND and Inclusion: Schools That Work for All Learners*. Oxon: Routledge.

Boddison, A. and Curran, H. (2022) The experience of SENCOs in England during the COVID-19 pandemic: The amplification and exposure of pre-existing strengths and challenges and the prioritisation of mental health and wellbeing in schools. *Journal of Research in Special Educational Needs*, Vol. 22, No. 2, pp. 126–136.

Boddison, A. and Soan, S. (2021) The coproduction illusion: Considering the relative success rates and efficiency rates of securing an Education, Health and Care plan when requested by families or education professionals. *Journal of Special Educational Needs*, Vol. 22, No. 2, pp. 91–104.

Boland, H., DiSalvo, M., Fried, R., Woodworth, K.Y., Wilens, T., Faraone, S.V. and Biederman, J. (2020) A literature review and meta-analysis on the effects of ADHD medications on functional outcomes. *Journal of Psychiatric Research*, Vol. 123, pp. 21–30.

Booth, S. (2022) All heads should have a SENCo qualification, says minister. *Schools Week*. https://schoolsweek.co.uk/all-heads-should-have-a-senco-qualification-says-minister Accessed in January 2024.

Bosse, L., McCarthy, K., Whitington, J. and Bakopoulou, I. (2019) Increasing school staff's knowledge in identifying communication needs and recognising the natural progression of EAL acquisition. In Bakopoulou, I., Vivash, J., Wall, K., Brackenbury, G. and Dockrell, J. (eds) *Supporting Spoken Language in the Classroom: Case Studies*. https://discovery.ucl.ac.uk/id/eprint/10085375/1/SSLiC_case%20studies.pdf Accessed in January 2024.

Brewin, P. and Knowler, H. (2023) The role of the SENCo: An essential or an extra? In Knowler, H., Richards, H. and Brewster, S. (eds) *Developing Your Expertise as a SENCo: Leading Inclusive Practice*. St Albans: Critical Publishing.

Browning, K. (2016) Helping schools meet the needs of SEN pupils. *Education Business*. https://education-businessuk.net/features/helping-schools-meet-needs-sen-pupils Accessed in December 2023.

Carroll, C., Brackenbury, G., Lee, F., Esposito, R. and O'Brien, T. (2020) Professional supervision: Guidance for SENCOs and school leaders. *UCL Centre for Inclusive Education*. https://discovery.ucl.ac.uk/id/eprint/10090818/1/Carroll_SENCO%20Supervision%20Guidance%20February%202020.pdf Accessed in January 2024.

Clarke, A.L. and Done, E.J. (2021) Balancing pressures for SENCos as managers, leaders and advocates in the emerging context of the Covid-19 pandemic. *British Journal of Special Education*, Vol. 48, No. 2, pp. 157–174.

Curran, H. (2019a) Are good intentions enough? The role of the policy implementer during Educational Reform. *Practice*, Vol. 1, No. 1, pp. 88–89.

Curran, H. (2019b) 'The SEND Code of Practice has given me clout': A phenomenological study illustrating how SENCos managed the introduction of the SEND reforms. *British Journal of Special Education*, Vol. 46, No. 1, pp. 76–93.

Curran, H. (2019c) *How to Be a Brilliant SENCO: Practical Strategies for Developing and Leading Inclusive Provision*. London: Routledge.

Curran, H. and Boddison, A. (2021) 'It's the best job in the world, but one of the hardest, loneliest, most misunderstood roles in a school.' Understanding the complexity of the SENCO role post-SEND reform. *Journal of Research in Special Educational Needs*, Vol. 21, No. 1, pp. 39–48.

Curran, H., Maloney, H, Heavey, A. and Boddison, A. (2018) It's about time: The impact of SENCO workload on the professional and the school. www.bathspa.ac.uk/media/bathspaacuk/education-/research/senco-workload/SENCOWorkloadReport-FINAL2018.pdf Accessed in June 2023.

Curran, H., Maloney, H., Heavy, A. and Boddison, A. (2021) National SENCO Workforce Survey 2020: Supporting children and young people with SEN and their families during the Coronavirus (COVID-19) pandemic. A national survey of SENCOs. www.bathspa.ac.uk/media/bathspaacuk/projects/15432-National-SENCO-Workforce-Survey-2020-PAGES.pdf Accessed in January 2024.

DfE (1994) Code of Practice on the identification and assessment of special educational needs. https://files.eric.ed.gov/fulltext/ED385033.pdf Accessed in November 2023.

DfE (2023a) Special educational needs and disability: An analysis and summary of data sources: June 2023. https://assets.publishing.service.gov.uk/media/64930eef103ca6001303a3a6/Special_educational_needs_and_disability_an_analysis_and_summary_of_data_sources.pdf Accessed in January 2024.

DfE (2023b) Suspensions and permanent exclusions in England. https://explore-education-statistics.service.gov.uk/find-statistics/suspensions-and-permanent-exclusions-in-england. Accessed in January 2024.

DfE (2023c) GCSE results (Attainment 8). www.ethnicity-facts-figures.service.gov.uk/education-skills-and-training/11-to-16-years-old/gcse-results-attainment-8-for-children-aged-14-to-16-key-stage-4/latest/ Accessed in March 2024.

DfE (2023d) Statistics: Special educational needs (SEN). www.gov.uk/government/collections/statistics-special-educational-needs-sen Accessed in January 2024.

DfE (2023e) Special educational needs in England: Academic year 2022/23. https://explore-education-statistics.service.gov.uk/find-statistics/special-educational-needs-in-england Accessed in January 2024.

DfE and DoH (2015) SEND Code of Practice, January. www.gov.uk/government/publications/send-code-of-practice-0-to-25 Accessed in January 2024.

DfES (2001) Special educational needs: Code of Practice. https://assets.publishing.service.gov.uk/media/5a7cac22ed915d7c983bc342/special_educational_needs_code_of_practice.pdf Accessed in November 2023.

Dobson, G.J. and Douglas, G. (2020) Who would do that role? Understanding why teachers become SENCos through an ecological systems theory. *Educational Review*, Vol. 72, No. 3, pp. 298–318.

Entefly (2023) Two AI winters and 1 hot AI summer. *Entefly*. www.entefy.com/blog/2-ai-winters-and-1-hot-ai-summer Accessed in January 2024.

Farina, M. and Lavazza, A. (2023) ChatGPT in society: Emerging issues. *Frontiers in Artificial Intelligence*, Vol. 6. DOI: 10.3389/frai.2023.1130913.

Fazackerley, A. (2022) Government 'pushing England's universities out of teacher training' over leftwing politics. *The Guardian*. www.theguardian.com/education/2022/may/28/government-pushing-universities-out-of-teacher-training-over-leftwing-politics-say-leaders Accessed in January 2024.

Fitzgerald, J. and Radford, J. (2022) Leadership for inclusive special education: A qualitative exploration of SENCOs' and principals' experiences in secondary schools in Ireland. *International Journal of Inclusive Education*, Vol. 26, No. 10, pp. 992–1007.

Francis, A. (2012) Stigma in an era of medicalisation and anxious parenting: How proximity and culpability shape middle class parents' experiences of disgrace. *Sociology of Health and Illness*, Vol. 34, No. 6, pp. 927–942.

Fry, H. (2018) *Hello World: How to Be Human in the Age of the Machine*. London: Penguin.

Gedge, N. and Phillips, S. (2019) *The* chapter that nearly didn't get written. In Webster, R. (ed.) *Including Children and Young People with Special Educational Needs and Disabilities in Learning and Life*. Oxon: Routledge.

Gov UK (2014) Children and Families Act. www.legislation.gov.uk/ukpga/2014/6/contents/enacted Accessed in April 2023.

Gov UK (2023) Find open data. www.data.gov.uk/ Accessed in February 2024.

Graham, B., White, C., Edwards, A., Potter, S. and Street, C. (2019) School exclusion: A literature review on the continued disproportionate exclusion of certain children. www.somersetvirtualschool.co.uk/wp-content/uploads/2017/05/Timpson_review_of_school_exclusion_literature_review-Copy.pdf Accessed in January 2024.

Grauer, K. (1995) Beliefs of preservice teachers toward art education. PhD Thesis, Simon Fraser University. https://core.ac.uk/download/pdf/56371013.pdf Accessed in January 2024.

Gross, J. (2023) SEND: A label worth having? *TES*. www.tes.com/magazine/teaching-learning/specialist-sector/send-pupil-label-alternative Accessed in January 2024.

Hallet, F. and Hallet, G. (2010) *Transforming the Role of the SENCO: Achieving the National Award for SEN Coordination*. Maidenhead: Oxford University Press.

Hallet, F. and Hallet, G. (2017) *Transforming the Role of the SENCO* (2nd edition). London: Oxford University Press.

Hamilton, L. (2010) The boundary seesaw model: Good fences make for good neighbours. In *Using Time, Not Doing Time: Practitioner Perspectives on Personality Disorder and Risk*. London: Wiley.

Harpur, P. (2012) From disability to ability: Changing the phrasing of the debate. *Disability & Society*, Vol. 27, No. 3, pp. 325–337.

Harris, C. (2019) All teachers are Sendcos now. *TES*. www.tes.com/magazine/archive/all-teachers-are-sendcos-now Accessed in October 2023.

Heikkila, M. (2022) The viral AI avatar app Lensa undressed me – without my consent. *MIT Technology Review*. www.technologyreview.com/2022/12/12/1064751/the-viral-ai-avatar-app-lensa-undressed-me-without-my-consent/ Accessed in January 2024.

Hellawell, B. (2017) 'There is still a long way to go to be solidly marvellous': Professional identities, performativity and responsibilisation arising from the SEND Code of Practice 2015. *British Journal of Special Education*, Vol. 44, No. 4, pp. 411–430.

Hewitt, D. and Tarrant, S. (2015) *Innovative Teaching and Learning in Primary Schools*. London: SAGE.

HM Government (2008) The Education (Special Educational Needs Co-ordinators) (England) Regulations 2008. www.legislation.gov.uk/uksi/2008/2945/made Accessed in December 2023.

HM Government (2022) SEND Review: Right support, right place, right time. Government Consultation on the SEND and alternative provision system in England. https://assets.publishing.service.gov.uk/media/624178c68fa8f5277c0168e7/SEND_review_right_support_right_place_right_time_accessible.pdf Accessed in January 2024.

HMSO (1993) Education Act 1993. www.legislation.gov.uk/ukpga/1993/35/pdfs/ukpga_19930035_en.pdf Accessed in January 2024.

Howieson, L., Huthwaite, K. and Knowler, H. (2023) SENCos using data to support inclusive practice. In Knowler, H., Richards, H. and Brewster, S. (eds) *Developing Your Expertise as a SENCo: Leading Inclusive Practice*. St Albans: Critical Publishing.

Huthwaite, K. and Howieson, L. (2023) The SENCo as an advocate. In Knowler, H., Richards, H. and Brewster, S. (eds) *Developing Your Expertise as a SENCo: Leading Inclusive Practice*. St Albans: Critical Publishing.

IFS (2023) Schools: The government has chosen to increase school spending in England at recent spending reviews. *Institute for Fiscal Studies*. https://ifs.org.uk/education-spending/schools Accessed in January 2024.

Ipsos (2023) Gen AI goes mainstream. *The Ipsos Almanac*. www.ipsos.com/en/almanac-2024/gen-ai-goes-mainstream Accessed in January 2024.

Johnson, M. and Coleman, V. (2023) Teaching in uncertain times: Exploring links between the pandemic, assessment workload, and teacher wellbeing in England. *Research in Education*. DOI: 10.1177/00345237231195270.

Johnstone, L. and Boyle, M. with Cromby, J., Dillon, J., Harper, D., Kinderman, P., Longden, E., Pilgrim, D. and Read, J. (2018) The power threat meaning framework: Overview. *British Psychological Society*. www.bps.org.uk/guideline/power-threat-meaning-framework-overview-version Accessed in March 2024.

Jones, G., Stead, J. and Kendrick, A. (2003) Joined-up approaches to prevent school exclusion. *Emotional and Behavioural Difficulties*, Vol. 8, No. 1, pp. 77–92.

Kearns, H. (2005) Exploring the experiential learning of special educational needs coordinators. *Journal of In-Service Education*, Vol. 31, No. 1, pp. 131–150.

King, H. (2016) The connection between personal traumas and educational exclusion in young people's lives. *Young*, Vol. 24, No. 4, pp. 342–358. DOI: 10.1177/1103308815627752.

Kirby, P. (2020) Dyslexia debated, then and now: A historical perspective on the dyslexia debate. *Oxford Review of Education*, Vol. 46, No. 4, pp. 472–486.

Klasen, S. (2001) Social exclusion, children and education: Conceptual and measurement issues. *OECD*. www.oecd.org/education/school/1855901.pdf Accessed in March 2024.

Klein, G. (2007) Performing a project premortem. *Harvard Business Review*. https://hbr.org/2007/09/performing-a-project-premortem Accessed in January 2024.

Knowler, H., Richards, H. and Brewster, S. (2023) *Developing Your Expertise as a SENCo: Leading Inclusive Practice*. St Albans: Critical Publishing.

Koplin, J. and Hatherley, J. (2022) It has become possible to use cutting-edge AI language models to generate convincing high school and undergraduate essays. Here's why that matters. *Practical Ethics (University of Oxford)*. https://blog.practicalethics.ox.ac.uk/2022/12/guest-post-it-has-become-possible-to-use-cutting-edge-ai-~language-models-to-generate-convincing-high-school-and-undergraduate-essays-heres-why-that-matters/ Accessed in January 2024.

Lamb, B. (2021) The future of SEND legislation in England: What next? In Beaton, M.C., Codina, G.N. and Wharton, J.C. (eds) *Leading on Inclusion: The Role of the SENCO*. Abingdon: Routledge, pp. 35–44.

Layton, L. (2005) Special educational needs coordinators and leadership: A role too far? *Support for Learning*, Vol. 20, No. 2, pp. 53–60.

Leeuw, R.R. de, Boer, A.A. de and Minnaert, A.E.M.G. (2018) Student voices on social exclusion in general primary schools. *European Journal of Special Needs Education*, Vol. 33, No. 2, pp. 166–186.

Lewis, A. and Norwich, B. (2005) *Special Teaching for Special Children? A Pedagogies for Inclusion*. Maidenhead: Open University Press.

Lindner, K.T., Hassani, S., Schwab, S., Gerdenitsch, C., Kopp-Sixt, S. and Holzinger, A. (2022) Promoting factors of social inclusion of students with special educational needs: Perspectives of parents, teachers and students. *Frontiers in Education*, Vol. 7. DOI: 10.3389/feduc.2022.773230.

Lindner, K.T. and Schwab, S. (2020) Differentiation and individualisation in inclusive education: A systematic review and narrative synthesis. *International Journal of Inclusive Education*. DOI: 10.1080/13603116.2020.1813450.

Malvania, U. and Majumdar, R. (2023) Businesses testing ways to safeguard against AI hallucination. *The Economic Times*. https://economictimes.indiatimes.com/tech/technology/businesses-testing-ways-to-safeguard-against-ai-hallucination/articleshow/105029934.cms Accessed in January 2024.

Mandinach, E. and Gummer, E. (2016) What does it mean for teachers to be data literate: Laying out the skills, knowledge, and dispositions. *Teaching and Teacher Education*, Vol. 60, pp. 366–376.

McKendrick, J. (2018) Artificial intelligence will replace tasks, not jobs. *Forbes*. www.forbes.com/sites/joemckendrick/2018/08/14/artificial-intelligence-will-replace-tasks-not-jobs/ Accessed in January 2024.

McWilliam, A. and Toner, F. (2021) Safe Space: How psychological safety can make your team more effective. *Forbes*. www.forbes.com/sites/googlecloud/2021/08/27/safe-space-how-psychological-safety-can-make-your-team-more-effective/?sh=622500d84231 Accessed in November 2023.

Middleton, T. and Kay, L. (2020) *Using an Inclusive Approach to Reduce School Exclusion: A Practitioner's Handbook*. London: Routledge.

Middleton, T. and Kay, L. (2021) Unchartered territory and extraordinary times: The SENCo's experiences of leading special education during a pandemic in England. *British Journal of Special Education*, Vol. 48, No. 2, pp. 212–234.

Morewood, G. (2018a) Corporate responsibility. In Bartram, D. (ed.) *Great Expectations: Leading an Effective SEND Strategy in School*. Woodbridge: John Catt.

Morewood, G. (2018b) Why we need more ethical SEND leaders. *The Optimus Blog*. https://blog.optimus-education.com/why-we-need-more-ethical-send-leaders Accessed in January 2024.

Nasen (n.d.) What is a SENCO. https://nasen.org.uk/page/what-senco Accessed in January 2024.

Norwich, B. (2013) *Addressing Tensions and Dilemmas in Inclusive Education: Living with uncertainty*. Oxon: Routledge.

O'Brien, J. (2016) *Don't Send Him in Tomorrow: Shining a Light on the Marginalised, Disenfranchised and Forgotten Children of Today's Schools*. Carmarthen: Independent Thinking Press.

ODI (2016) What is open data? *Open Data Institute*. https://theodi.org/news-and-events/blog/what-is-open-data/ Accessed in January 2024.

Oldham, J. and Radford, J. (2011) Secondary SENCo leadership: A universal or specialist role? *British Journal of Special Education*, Vol. 38, No. 3, pp. 126–134.

Packer, N. (2014) *The Perfect SENCO*. Carmarthen: Independent Thinking Press.

Parkes, B. (2012) Exclusion of pupils from school in the UK. *The Equal Rights Review*, Vol. 8. www.equalrightstrust.org/ertdocumentbank/ERR8_Brenda_Parkes.pdf Accessed in February 2024.

Peacock, A. (2018) Teaching and learning. In Bartram, D. (ed.) *Great Expectations: Leading an Effective SEND Strategy in School*. Woodbridge: John Catt.

Pickles, D. (2023) Analysing data for pupils with SEND. *Sensible SENCO*. www.sensiblesenco.org.uk/analysing-data-for-pupils-with-send/ Accessed in January 2024.

Purdy, N. and Boddison, A. (2018) Special educational needs and inclusion. In Cremin, T. and Burnett, C. (eds) *Learning to Teach in the Primary School*. London: Routledge.

Richards, H., Hall, H., Wells, J. and Stuart, Z. (2023) The SENCo role across ages and settings. In Knowler, H., Richards, H. and Brewster, S. (eds) *Developing Your Expertise as a SENCo: Leading Inclusive Practice*. St Albans: Critical Publishing.

Richards, H. and Legarska, A. (2023) Critical reflection in professional practice. In Knowler, H., Richards, H. and Brewster, S. (eds) *Developing Your Expertise as a SENCo: Leading Inclusive Practice*. St Albans: Critical Publishing.

Roberts, T. and Marchais, G. (2018) Assessing the role of social media and digital technology in violence reporting. *Contemporary Readings in Law and Social Justice*, Vol. 10, No. 2, pp. 9–42.

Robinson, D., Moore, N. and Hooley, T. (2018) Ensuring an independent future for young people with special educational needs and disabilities (SEND): A critical examination of the impact of education, health and care plans in England. *British Journal of Guidance and Counselling*, Vol. 46, No. 4, pp. 479–491.

Ross, H. (2019) All teachers as SenCos? https://helensplace.co.uk/2019/07/08/all-teachers-as-sencos/ Accessed in October 2023.

Rozsahegyi, T. and Lambert, M. (2023) Pedagogy, inclusion and the SENCo's role. In Knowler, H., Richards, H. and Brewster, S. (eds) *Developing Your Expertise as a SENCo: Leading Inclusive Practice*. St Albans: Critical Publishing.

Savva, N. (2020) The world is data-rich but analysis poor: Why business needs a fresh approach to unlocking the value of data. *Think (London Business School)*. www.london.edu/think/the-world-is-data-rich-but-analysis-poor Accessed in January 2024.

Scaglione, I. (2021) The efficacy and ethical issues of ADHD medication in young child. *Digital Commons at Sacred Heart University*. https://digitalcommons.sacredheart.edu/cgi/viewcontent.cgi?article=1604&context=acadfest Accessed in February 2024.

Silva, M. and Portman, H. (2019) Creatures that slow down portfolio delivery and how to kill them. *PM World Journal*, Vol. 8, No. 9. https://pmworldlibrary.net/wp-content/uploads/2019/10/pmwj86-Oct2019-Silva-Portman-creatures-that-slow-portfolio-delivery.pdf Accessed in February 2024.

Sjostrom, D., Rask, O., Welin, L., Petersson, M.G., Gustafsson, P., Landgren, K. and Eberhard, S. (2023) The winding road to equal care: Attitudes and experiences of prescribing ADHD medication among pediatric psychiatrists: A qualitative study. *International Journal of Environmental Research and Public Health*, Vol. 20, No. 1, Article 221. DOI: 10.3390/ijerph20010221.

Smith, A (2022a) "Why should I worry . . . the SENCO will do it all": Recognising the importance of the Special Educational Needs Coordinator (SENCO) in our schools in readiness for a post-covid-19 world. http://nectar.northampton.ac.uk/17375/1/Smith_Andy_Routledge_2022_Why_should_I_worry_the_SENCO_will_do_it_all.pdf Accessed in January 2024.

Smith, A. (2022b) The experiences of new primary school special educational needs coordinators: Presenting the SENCO voice through concept-drawing and personal narratives. *Support for Learning*, Vol. 37, No. 1, pp. 91–97.

Smith, M.D. and Broomhead, K.E. (2019) Time, expertise and status: Barriers faced by mainstream primary school SENCos in the pursuit of providing effective provision for children with SEND. *Support for Learning*, Vol. 34, No. 1, pp. 54–70.

Soan, S. and Monsen, J. (2023) *Inclusive Education Theory and Policy: Moving from Special Educational Needs to Equity*. Maidenhead: Open University Press.

Sobel, D. (2018) *Narrowing the Attainment Gap: A Handbook for Schools*. London: Bloomsbury.

Stobbs, P. (2023) High Tides, Pudding Lane and a Curious Child. Valedictory Address at Portcullis House, PowerPoint Presentation.

Taylor, C. (2018) Efficient use of resources. In Bartram (ed.) *Great Expectations: Leading an Effective SEND Strategy in School*. Woodbridge: John Catt.

TES (2022) How do school budgets work? *Times Educational Supplement*. www.tes.com/magazine/analysis/specialist-sector/how-do-school-budgets-work Accessed in January 2024.

The Key (2022) School budget: Expenditure on staffing. *The Key*. https://schoolleaders.thekeysupport.com/administration-and-management/financial-management/budget/school-budget-expenditure-on-staffing/ Accessed in January 2024.

Thorpe, H. (2023) ChatGPT is fun, but not an author. *Science (AAAS)*, Vol. 379, No. 6630. DOI: 10.1126/science.adg7879

Tirraoro, T. (2018) The devastating impact of the SENCO workload. *Special Needs Jungle*. www.special-needsjungle.com/the-devastating-impact-of-the-senco-workload/ Accessed in December 2023.

Tissot, C. (2013) The role of SENCos as leaders. *British Journal of Special Education*, Vol. 40, No. 1, pp. 33–40.

Tsai, Y., Perrotta, C. and Gasevic, D. (2020) Empowering learners with personalised learning approaches? Agency, equity and transparency in the context of learning analytics. *Assessment and Evaluation in Higher Education*, Vol. 45, No. 4, pp. 554–567.

TTA (1998) *National Standards for Special Educational Needs Coordinators*. London: Teacher Training Agency.

Tutt, R. (2011) *Partnership Working to Support Special Educational Needs and Disabilities*. London: SAGE.

Tutt, R. (2016a) *Rona Tutt's Guide to SEND and Inclusion*. London: Sage.

Tutt, R. (2016b) The job of a SENCO is to change a school's culture. *Teachwire*. www.teachwire.net/news/the-job-of-a-senco-is-to-change-a-schools-culture/ Accessed in December 2023.

United Nations (1989) Convention on the rights of the child. www.unicef.org/child-rights-convention/convention-text Accessed in February 2024.

Vincent, M. (2022) The intricacies of strategic misrepresentation in project management. *Applied Change*. https://appliedchange.co.uk/why-do-we-lie/ Accessed in December 2023.

Walker, A. (2023) Teacher training ditched by unis with 90 years' experience: Four providers unsuccessful in the DfE's market review to close PGCE courses. *Schools Week*. https://schoolsweek.co.uk/teacher-training-ditched-by-universities-with-90-years-experience/ Accessed in December 2023.

Warnock, M. (1978) The Warnock report. www.educationengland.org.uk/documents/warnock/warnock1978.html Accessed in November 2019.

Wedell, K. (2019) Recognising paradigm shifts. In Webster, R. (ed.) *Including Children and Young People with Special Educational Needs and Disabilities in Learning and Life*. Oxon: Routledge.

Yates, D. and Boddison, A. (2020) *The School Handbook for Dual and Multiple Exceptionality: High Learning Potential with Special Educational Needs or Disabilities*. London: Routledge.

Zeltser, F. (2021) A psychologist shares the four styles of parenting – and the type that researchers say is the most successful. *CNBC: Make It*. www.cnbc.com/2021/06/29/child-psychologist-explains-4-types-of-parenting-and-how-to-tell-which-is-right-for-you.html Accessed in February 2024.

# Index

Note: Page numbers in *italics* indicate a figure and page numbers in **bold** indicate a table on the corresponding page.

academic exclusion 43–44
antecedent 29–30
artificial intelligence (AI) 31, 50, 62; hallucination 69; replacing tasks, not roles 72; in schools 69–73
Attachment and Trauma Response Care Framework 35
Autism Spectrum Disorder (ASD) 10, 34, 51, 55, 81

basic formulae, Excel 62–63, *63*
behaviour: as communication 88–89; consequences 93–94; management and parenting 33–34
benefit of hindsight, SENCOs: career development 76; extra mile 79; getting stuck 75–76; practical and tactical advice 76–78
Browning, K. 15
'built-in': movement breaks, into the lesson 30; opportunities for repair built into lunchtimes 43
built-in accessibility tools 31, 63

Changing Minds Child and Family Services (CMCAFS) 37
ChatGPT 73; accessibility 72; bias and bullying 73; curriculum diversity 73; evaluate and adjust 73; families and communities 73; inclusive language and communication 72; inclusive policies 72; promoting diversity 72; safe spaces creation 72; training staff 72; to write a SEND strategy 70–71
Children and Families Act 7, 16
Clarke, A. L. 6
Code of Practice *see* SEND Code of Practice
communication: behaviour as 19, 27, 28, 38, 88–89; inclusive language and 72; visuals for 57–60, *59–61*
conditional formatting, Excel 62, 67, *67*, 68
continuing professional development (CPD) 28, 30, 34, 53, 76
coproduction 8, 16, 40, 94
coproduction illusion 85, 90
Curran, H. 4, 7, 13

data 19, 49, 52–55, **53–54**, *54*
data for delivery: artificial intelligence (AI), schools 69–73; BRAG rating 68; data literacy for SENCOs 56–68; data sources for SEND 55; data usage by SENCOs 50–55; RAG report 68; routine data analysis 49; watermelon reporting 69
data literacy for SENCOs: average increase in reading age 58–59, **59**; basics of Excel 62–68; data discussion 60–62, *61*; data familiarisation 57; fundamental misconception 56; learning, unlearning and relearning 62; pre- and post-literacy intervention **58**; steps *57*; visuals for communication 57–60, *59–61*
data usage by SENCOs: Apples and Pears 56; data sets for SEND identification 55; Gov.UK Open Data Hub 56; provision maps 56; SEND identification data 52–55, **53**, **54**, *54*
Department for Education (DfE) 17, 19, 27, 52
deputy SENCO, appointing 83
designated safeguarding lead (DSL) 11, 12, 76, 80
Developmental Language Disorder (DLD) 87
digital dictionaries 31
disruptive behaviour, persistent 21–22
Dobson, G. J. 5
Done, E. J. 6
Douglas, G. 5

Early Career Teacher (ECT) 5, 88
EHC plan 2, 27, 34, 43, 55, 86
equality and equity 45–47
Equality, diversity and inclusion (EDI) 45
ethics 8–11, 69, 73
Excel basics: conditional formatting *67*, 67–68; creating graphs 63–64, *64*, *65*; filters 64–66, *65*; sorting lists 66, 66–67; using basic formulae 62–63, *63*
exclusion 19, 47–48: academic 43–44; behaviour management and parenting 33–34; class teams 29–33; developing school's approach 28–29; equality and equity 45–47; Four Rs approach *38*, 38–39; Headteacher red lines 26–28; HEARTS framework 37; Hope School approach 34–36; inclusion tactics 29; national situation 19–21, *20*, *21*; Nisai approach 43–47; permanent exclusions 20, *20*; primary school case studies 42–43; responding to immediate situation 22, 22–26; SENCO perspective 21–22; with SEND 20, *20*; social 44–45; stakeholder perspectives 40–41; suspensions 20, *20*, *21*; zero-exclusion 37–40

filters, Excel 64, *65*
The Four/4 Rs 38–39, *38*
Froehle, C. 36
Fry, H. 73

governor *see* SEND governor
graphs, Excel 63–64, *64–65*
Gummer, E. 57

Headteacher Red Lines 26–28
HEARTS programme 35
Hewitt, D. 8
Hope School approach 34–36; Four Rs approach *38*, 38–39; HEARTS framework 37; overview 34–35; relational policy 38; zero exclusions 37–40
Howieson, L. 57

inclusion 9–11, 85; ChatGPT created SEND strategy for 70–71; duties and responsibilities of SEND governor 15–16, 18; Equality, diversity and inclusion (EDI) 45; equality and equity 45–47; recognizing antecedents to inform inclusion tactics 29; relationship with colleagues 85; social exclusion and 44
inclusion tactics 29
Institute for Fiscal Studies 7

Kearns, H. 3
knowledge-centred curriculum 9

labelling 8–10, 40, 64, 76
leadership 6–8, 17, 60

Mandinach, E. 57
moderate learning difficulties (MLD) 10, 49, 55, 78
Morewood, G. 12
movement breaks 30

National Association for Special Educational Needs (nasen) 1, 12, 14
Nisai approach: academic exclusion 43–44; breakdown of needs 46, *46*; equality and equity 45–47; SEND and TD learners 46; social exclusion 44–45
Norwich, B. 9

O'Brien, J. 13
Open Data Hub 56
Open Data Institute (ODI) 56
ordinarily-available provision 9–11, 17, 26, 30, 36, *37*

parenting styles *33*
passion and politeness 79–80
Peacock, A. 3
Pickles, D. 60
policy 27, 34, 37, 84
power and interest matrix 24, *25*, 32
Power Threat Meaning Framework 25
pre-mortems 31–32

primary school 7–8, 9; case studies 42–43, 79–80
Purdy, N. 14

quality-first teaching 8, 9, 14, 26
Quince, W. 11

RACI matrix 2, 32, **33**
'red lines' 26; Headteacher 26–28; stakeholders 40–43
reporting by exception 68, 73
relationships 13, 23, 75, 84; between school and home 91–96; with colleagues 85, 88–89; in general 84; with hard-to-reach families 78–79; *Healthy relationship with ourselves and with our peers* (free resource) 96; 'Hope school' approach 34–35, 38, 39; online, with 'Nisai approach' 46; with parents and carers 84–85, 87, 88; zero exclusion strategies and 39–40
risk: AI and 69–70; dynamic risk assessment 23–24, 26; identifying and mitigating 31–32; of overlooking data 49; reduced level of risk-taking 42

school exclusions *see* exclusion
*The School Exclusions Hub* 48
*The School Exclusions video guide for caregivers* 48
SENCO National Professional Qualification (NPQ) 1, 17
SENCO Regulations 3, 15
SENCO role: benefit of hindsight 75–80; case studies 87; data literacy for 56–68; depth, breadth and reach 12–13; description of 1–2; developments of 17; Early Career Teacher (ECT) 5; ethics 8–9; evolution of 2–3; good intentions 88; leaning on family and colleagues 80; mindset 81; Ofsted inspections 86–87; pastoral leaders/drivers 8; phase-specific variations 7–8; practical advice for 87–88; professional support and clinical supervision 80–81; responsibilities 4; school budgets 7; SEND expertise 10–11; SEND Governor 14–17; statutory guidance 1; statutory requirements 14; strategic leaders 6–7; teachers 5–6; teaching and learning perspectives 8; work-life balance 82–84; workload and administration 4–5
SEND: administration 77–78; ChatGPT 70–71; data sets for identification 55; definition of 9, 10; disproportionate number of pupils 8; equality, equity and liberation 36, *36*; expertise 10–11; perceptions of 35–36; pre-mortems 31–32; proportion of learners **53**; register 78–79; trauma-informed approaches 81
SEND Code of Practice 2–4, 6–7, 11, 13–16, 51, 86
SEND governor 3, 4, 14–17, 51, 52, 88; role description 15–17
SEND magnet 13–14
SEN policy 1, 2, 4
social exclusion 44–45

sorting lists, Excel 62, 66
speech, language and communication needs
    (SLCN) 12, 20, 55
stakeholders: child 40–41; community engagement
    71; engagement 24–26; identification 32, **33**;
    parents and carers 41; relationships 84; school
    community 41; staff 41
Stobbs, P. 36
strategic misrepresentation 50, 69, 73

Tarrant, S. 8
*The Teacher Handbook: SEND* 18
Teacher Training Agency (TTA) 2
trauma-informed approach 34–35, 78, 81

trauma-responsive approach 31, 34, 35
Tutt, R. 7

University College London (UCL) Centre for
    inclusive education 31, 90

'vital for some, valuable for all' approach 30, 31

Warnock Report 2
watermelon reporting 50, 68–69
Whole School SEND 2, 5, 6, 10–12, 14
workload 4–6, 13, 49

Zeltser, F. 13
zero exclusions 37–40